Gifts from a Jar Kids' Treats

Gift Giving Made Easy

Show your friends and family just how much you care by giving them a beautiful homemade gift jar filled with the ingredients to make delicious and fun kids' treats.

Keep the following tips in mind when preparing your gift jars:

- Always use a food-safe jar or container with an airtight lid. Make sure the jar or container is completely clean and dry before filling it with ingredients.
- Use the jar size called for in the recipe.
- Measure all the ingredients accurately.
- For ease in filling, use a wide-mouth jar if possible. Layer the ingredients into the jar using a ¼ cup dry measuring cup or the largest spoon that fits through the mouth of the jar.
- For more attractive jars, divide ingredients with large amounts (1 cup or more) into two layers.
- Fine ingredients, such as flour and granulated sugar, are best layered at the bottom of the jar, or on top of more compact ingredients, such as oats and brown sugar.
- Use small sandwich bags to hold ingredients as directed in some mix recipes. Close the bag with a twist tie, then cut off the top of the bag before placing it in the jar.
- After the jar is filled, make sure to replace the lid securely. Then, tear out the corresponding gift tag from this book. Cover the top of the jar with a 9- or 10-inch circle of fabric. Attach the fabric and the gift tag onto the jar with raffia, ribbon, satin cord, string or lace.

Granola Cookie Mix

¾ cup all-purpose flour
½ teaspoon salt
½ teaspoon baking soda
½ teaspoon ground cinnamon
¾ cup packed brown sugar
1 cup granola cereal
¾ cup semisweet chocolate chips
¾ cup raisins

Layer ingredients in 1-quart food storage jar with tight-fitting lid in following order: combined flour, salt, baking soda and cinnamon; brown sugar, lightly packed; granola; chocolate chips; and raisins. Seal jar; cover lid with fabric. Attach gift tag and fabric to jar with raffia.

Makes one 1-quart jar

Granola Cookies

½ cup (1 stick) butter, softened
1 egg
1 jar Granola Cookie Mix
1 tablespoon milk

1. Preheat oven to 350°F. Grease cookie sheets; set aside.

2. Beat butter in large bowl 1 minute with electric mixer at medium speed. Add egg; beat until well blended. Add contents of jar and milk; beat on low speed until well blended.

3. Drop dough by rounded tablespoonfuls 1½ inches apart onto prepared cookie sheets. Bake 10 to 12 minutes or until cookies are firm and lightly browned. Cool 2 minutes on cookie sheets; remove to wire rack. Cool completely. *Makes about 3 dozen cookies*

Granola Cookies

½ cup (1 stick) butter, softened
1 egg
1 jar Granola Cookie Mix
1 tablespoon milk

1. Preheat oven to 350°F. Grease cookie sheets; set aside.
2. Beat butter in large bowl 1 minute with electric mixer at medium speed. Add egg; beat until well blended. Add contents of jar and milk; beat on low speed until well blended.
3. Drop dough by rounded tablespoonfuls 1½ inches apart onto prepared cookie sheets. Bake 10 to 12 minutes or until cookies are firm and lightly browned. Cool 2 minutes on cookie sheets; remove to wire rack. Cool completely.

Makes about 3 dozen cookies

Granola Cookies

½ cup (1 stick) butter, softened
1 egg
1 jar Granola Cookie Mix
1 tablespoon milk

1. Preheat oven to 350°F. Grease cookie sheets; set aside.
2. Beat butter in large bowl 1 minute with electric mixer at medium speed. Add egg; beat until well blended. Add contents of jar and milk; beat on low speed until well blended.
3. Drop dough by rounded tablespoonfuls 1½ inches apart onto prepared cookie sheets. Bake 10 to 12 minutes or until cookies are firm and lightly browned. Cool 2 minutes on cookie sheets; remove to wire rack. Cool completely.

Makes about 3 dozen cookies

Granola Cookies

½ cup (1 stick) butter, softened
1 egg
1 jar Granola Cookie Mix
1 tablespoon milk

1. Preheat oven to 350°F. Grease cookie sheets; set aside.
2. Beat butter in large bowl 1 minute with electric mixer at medium speed. Add egg; beat until well blended. Add contents of jar and milk; beat on low speed until well blended.
3. Drop dough by rounded tablespoonfuls 1½ inches apart onto prepared cookie sheets. Bake 10 to 12 minutes or until cookies are firm and lightly browned. Cool 2 minutes on cookie sheets; remove to wire rack. Cool completely.

Makes about 3 dozen cookies

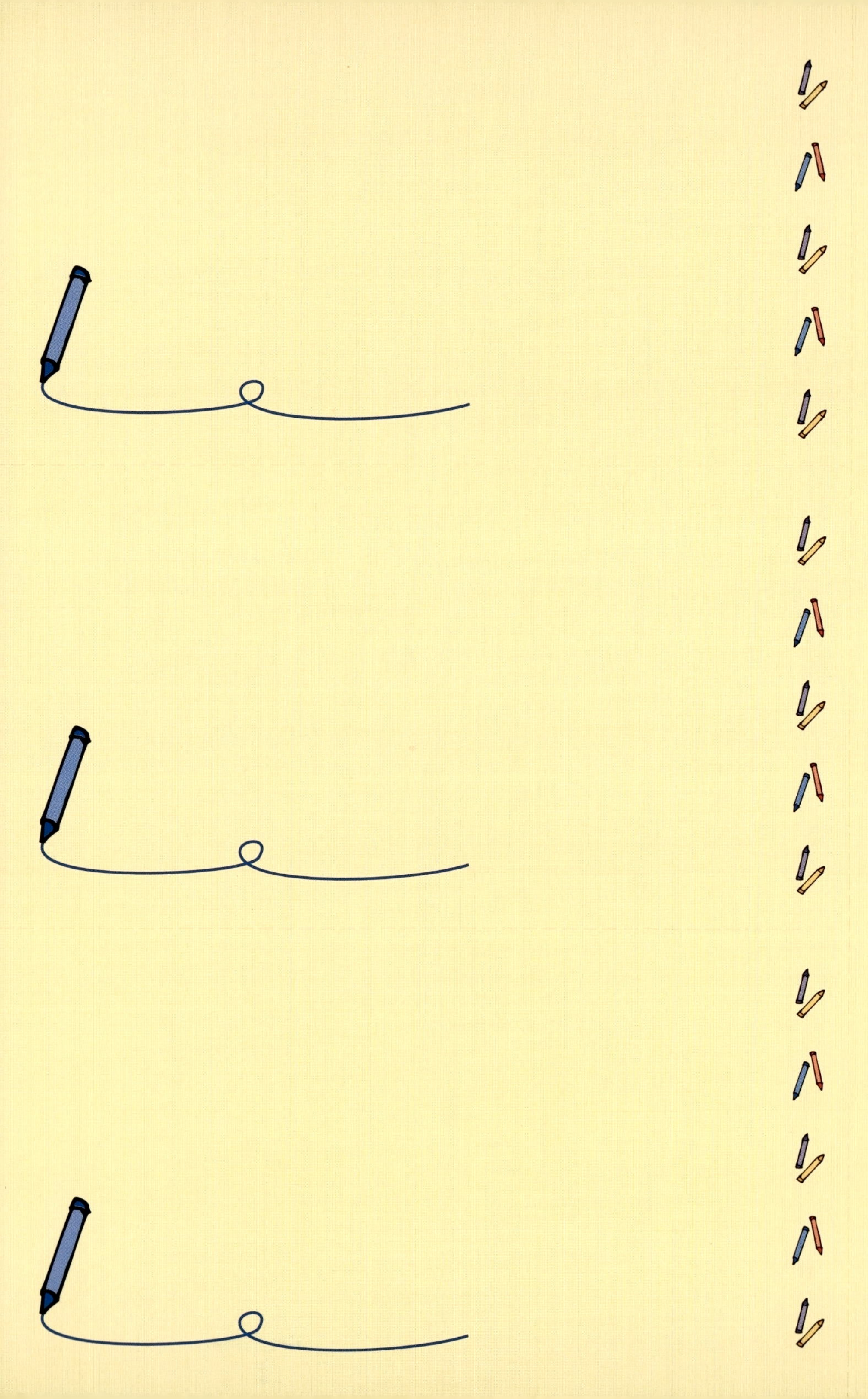

Granola Cookies

½ cup (1 stick) butter, softened
1 egg
1 jar Granola Cookie Mix
1 tablespoon milk

1. Preheat oven to 350°F. Grease cookie sheets; set aside.

2. Beat butter in large bowl 1 minute with electric mixer at medium speed. Add egg; beat until well blended. Add contents of jar and milk; beat on low speed until well blended.

3. Drop dough by rounded tablespoonfuls 1½ inches apart onto prepared cookie sheets. Bake 10 to 12 minutes or until cookies are firm and lightly browned. Cool 2 minutes on cookie sheets; remove to wire rack. Cool completely.

Makes about 3 dozen cookies

Granola Cookies

½ cup (1 stick) butter, softened
1 egg
1 jar Granola Cookie Mix
1 tablespoon milk

1. Preheat oven to 350°F. Grease cookie sheets; set aside.

2. Beat butter in large bowl 1 minute with electric mixer at medium speed. Add egg; beat until well blended. Add contents of jar and milk; beat on low speed until well blended.

3. Drop dough by rounded tablespoonfuls 1½ inches apart onto prepared cookie sheets. Bake 10 to 12 minutes or until cookies are firm and lightly browned. Cool 2 minutes on cookie sheets; remove to wire rack. Cool completely.

Makes about 3 dozen cookies

Granola Cookies

½ cup (1 stick) butter, softened
1 egg
1 jar Granola Cookie Mix
1 tablespoon milk

1. Preheat oven to 350°F. Grease cookie sheets; set aside.

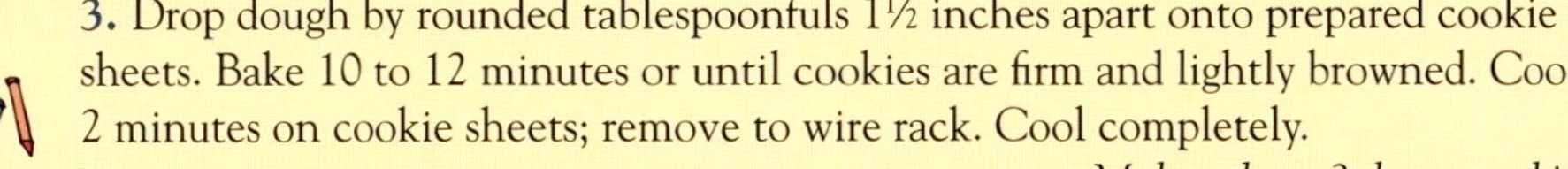

2. Beat butter in large bowl 1 minute with electric mixer at medium speed. Add egg; beat until well blended. Add contents of jar and milk; beat on low speed until well blended.

3. Drop dough by rounded tablespoonfuls 1½ inches apart onto prepared cookie sheets. Bake 10 to 12 minutes or until cookies are firm and lightly browned. Cool 2 minutes on cookie sheets; remove to wire rack. Cool completely.

Makes about 3 dozen cookies

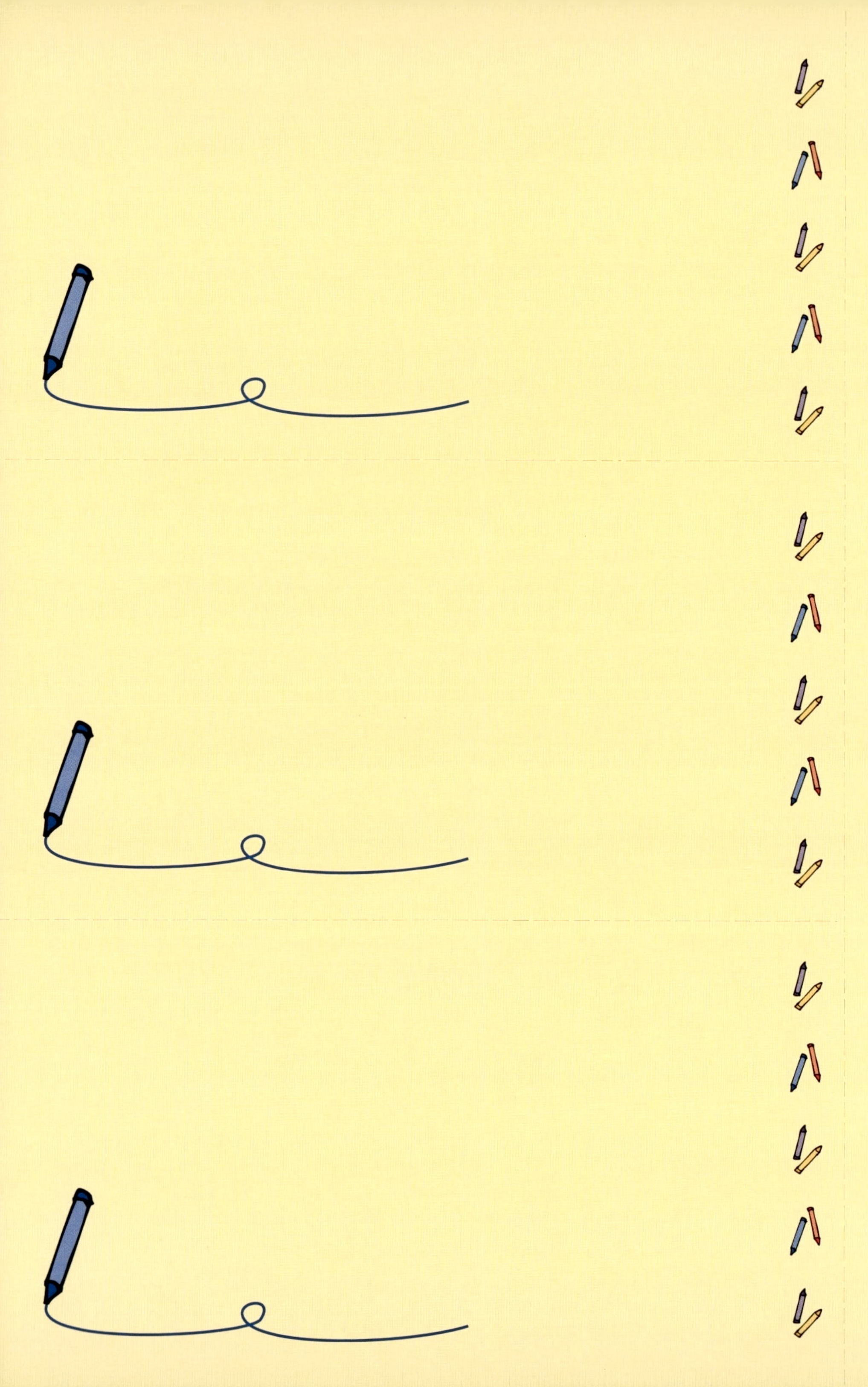

Mint Surprise Brownie Mix

- ⅔ cup granulated sugar
- ¾ cup packed brown sugar
- 1 cup all-purpose flour
- ½ teaspoon baking powder
- ½ teaspoon salt
- ⅔ cup unsweetened cocoa powder
- 1 cup chocolate-covered bite-size mint candies

Layer ingredients in 1-quart food storage jar with tight-fitting lid in following order: granulated sugar; brown sugar, lightly packed; combined flour, baking powder and salt; cocoa; and candies in small plastic bag. Seal jar; cover lid with fabric. Attach gift tag and fabric to jar with raffia.

Makes one 1-quart jar

Mint Surprise Brownies

1 cup (2 sticks) butter
1 jar Mint Surprise Brownie Mix
3 eggs, slightly beaten
1 teaspoon vanilla
Chocolate frosting (optional)

1. Preheat oven to 350°F. Grease 13×9-inch baking pan.

2. Place butter in large microwavable bowl. Microwave at HIGH 1 to 1½ minutes or until butter is just melted. Cool slightly.

3. Remove bag of candies from jar; set aside. Add remaining contents of jar, eggs and vanilla to butter; stir until well blended.

4. Stir in candies. Spread batter into prepared pan. Bake 30 to 32 minutes or until toothpick inserted into center comes out clean. Cool completely in pan on wire rack. Frost, if desired. Cut into bars.

Makes 24 brownies

Mint Surprise Brownies

1 cup (2 sticks) butter
1 jar Mint Surprise Brownie Mix
3 eggs, slightly beaten
1 teaspoon vanilla
Chocolate frosting (optional)

1. Preheat oven to 350°F. Grease 13×9-inch baking pan.
2. Place butter in large microwavable bowl. Microwave at HIGH 1 to 1½ minutes or until butter is just melted. Cool slightly.
3. Remove bag of candies from jar; set aside. Add remaining contents of jar, eggs and vanilla to butter; stir until well blended.
4. Stir in candies. Spread batter into prepared pan. Bake 30 to 32 minutes or until toothpick inserted into center comes out clean. Cool completely in pan on wire rack. Frost, if desired. Cut into bars. *Makes 24 brownies*

Mint Surprise Brownies

1 cup (2 sticks) butter
1 jar Mint Surprise Brownie Mix
3 eggs, slightly beaten
1 teaspoon vanilla
Chocolate frosting (optional)

1. Preheat oven to 350°F. Grease 13×9-inch baking pan.
2. Place butter in large microwavable bowl. Microwave at HIGH 1 to 1½ minutes or until butter is just melted. Cool slightly.
3. Remove bag of candies from jar; set aside. Add remaining contents of jar, eggs and vanilla to butter; stir until well blended.
4. Stir in candies. Spread batter into prepared pan. Bake 30 to 32 minutes or until toothpick inserted into center comes out clean. Cool completely in pan on wire rack. Frost, if desired. Cut into bars. *Makes 24 brownies*

Mint Surprise Brownies

1 cup (2 sticks) butter
1 jar Mint Surprise Brownie Mix
3 eggs, slightly beaten
1 teaspoon vanilla
Chocolate frosting (optional)

1. Preheat oven to 350°F. Grease 13×9-inch baking pan.
2. Place butter in large microwavable bowl. Microwave at HIGH 1 to 1½ minutes or until butter is just melted. Cool slightly.
3. Remove bag of candies from jar; set aside. Add remaining contents of jar, eggs and vanilla to butter; stir until well blended.
4. Stir in candies. Spread batter into prepared pan. Bake 30 to 32 minutes or until toothpick inserted into center comes out clean. Cool completely in pan on wire rack. Frost, if desired. Cut into bars. *Makes 24 brownies*

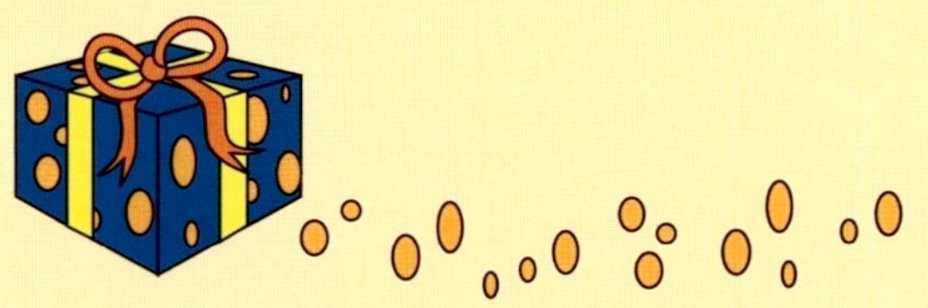

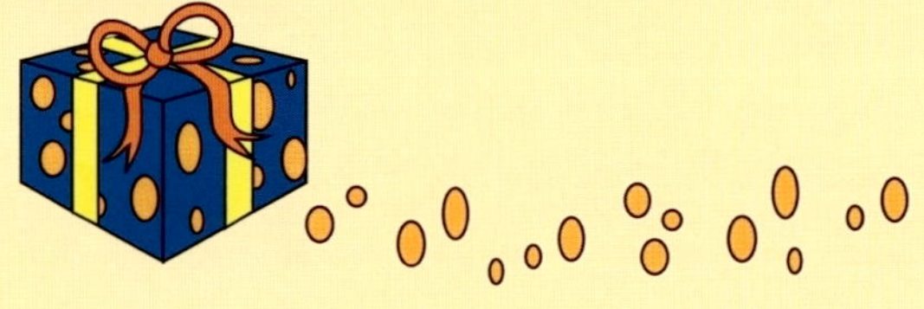

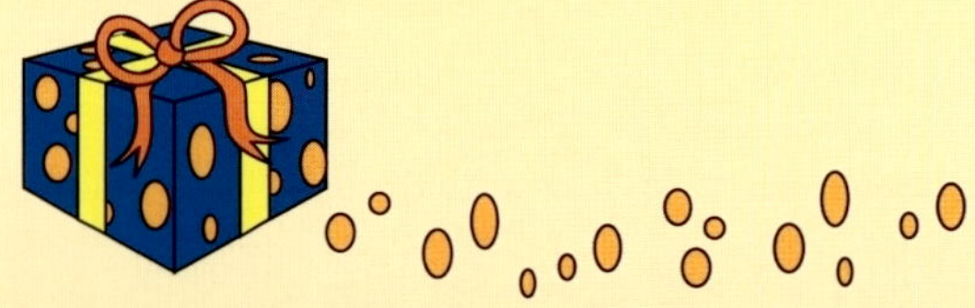

Mint Surprise Brownies

- **1 cup (2 sticks) butter**
- **1 jar Mint Surprise Brownie Mix**
- **3 eggs, slightly beaten**
- **1 teaspoon vanilla**
- **Chocolate frosting (optional)**

1. Preheat oven to 350°F. Grease 13×9-inch baking pan.
2. Place butter in large microwavable bowl. Microwave at HIGH 1 to 1½ minutes or until butter is just melted. Cool slightly.
3. Remove bag of candies from jar; set aside. Add remaining contents of jar, eggs and vanilla to butter; stir until well blended.
4. Stir in candies. Spread batter into prepared pan. Bake 30 to 32 minutes or until toothpick inserted into center comes out clean. Cool completely in pan on wire rack. Frost, if desired. Cut into bars.

Makes 24 brownies

Mint Surprise Brownies

- **1 cup (2 sticks) butter**
- **1 jar Mint Surprise Brownie Mix**
- **3 eggs, slightly beaten**
- **1 teaspoon vanilla**
- **Chocolate frosting (optional)**

1. Preheat oven to 350°F. Grease 13×9-inch baking pan.
2. Place butter in large microwavable bowl. Microwave at HIGH 1 to 1½ minutes or until butter is just melted. Cool slightly.
3. Remove bag of candies from jar; set aside. Add remaining contents of jar, eggs and vanilla to butter; stir until well blended.
4. Stir in candies. Spread batter into prepared pan. Bake 30 to 32 minutes or until toothpick inserted into center comes out clean. Cool completely in pan on wire rack. Frost, if desired. Cut into bars.

Makes 24 brownies

Mint Surprise Brownies

- **1 cup (2 sticks) butter**
- **1 jar Mint Surprise Brownie Mix**
- **3 eggs, slightly beaten**
- **1 teaspoon vanilla**
- **Chocolate frosting (optional)**

1. Preheat oven to 350°F. Grease 13×9-inch baking pan.
2. Place butter in large microwavable bowl. Microwave at HIGH 1 to 1½ minutes or until butter is just melted. Cool slightly.
3. Remove bag of candies from jar; set aside. Add remaining contents of jar, eggs and vanilla to butter; stir until well blended.
4. Stir in candies. Spread batter into prepared pan. Bake 30 to 32 minutes or until toothpick inserted into center comes out clean. Cool completely in pan on wire rack. Frost, if desired. Cut into bars.

Makes 24 brownies

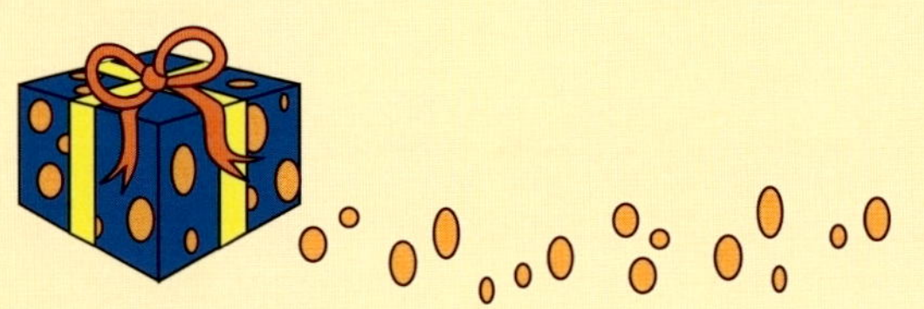

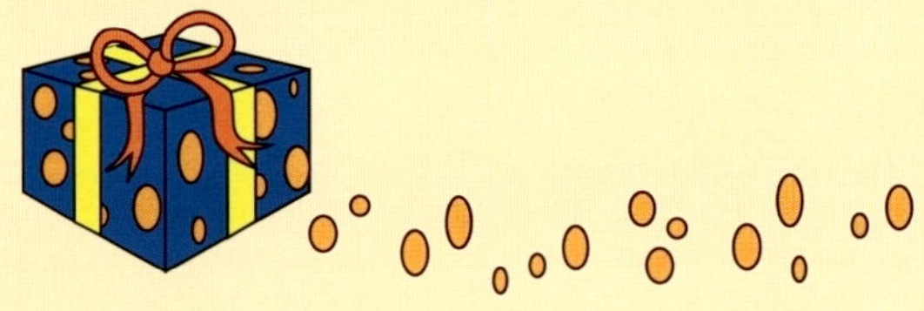

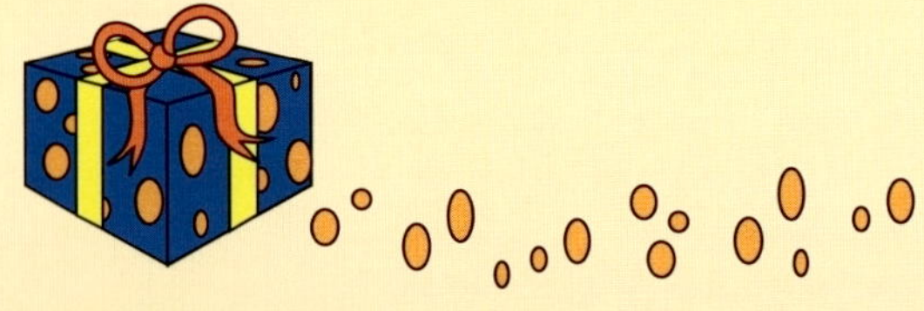

Easy Layered Bar Mix

½ cup candy-coated chocolate candies or baking bits
1 cup semisweet chocolate chips
1¼ cups crisp rice cereal
1 cup peanut butter chips
½ cup flaked coconut
1½ cups graham cracker crumbs

Layer ingredients in 1½-quart food storage jar with tight-fitting lid in following order: candies; chocolate chips; cereal; peanut butter chips; coconut; and graham cracker crumbs in plastic bag. Seal jar; cover lid with fabric. Attach gift tag and fabric to jar with raffia.

Makes one 1½-quart jar

Easy Layered Bars

½ cup (1 stick) butter or margarine, melted
1 can (14 ounces) sweetened condensed milk
1 jar Easy Layered Bar Mix

1. Preheat oven to 350°F. Lightly spray sides of 13×9-inch baking pan with nonstick cooking spray. Pour butter evenly into pan.

2. Remove graham cracker crumbs from jar and sprinkle over butter. Pour condensed milk evenly over crumbs. Carefully sprinkle coconut and peanut butter chips in even layers, then cereal, chocolate chips and candies; press gently.

3. Bake 25 to 27 minutes or until top just begins to brown. Cool completely in pan on wire rack. Cut into bars.

Makes about 36 bars

Easy Layered Bars

½ cup (1 stick) butter or margarine, melted

1 can (14 ounces) sweetened condensed milk

1 jar Easy Layered Bar Mix

1. Preheat oven to 350°F. Lightly spray sides of 13×9-inch baking pan with nonstick cooking spray. Pour butter evenly into pan.

2. Remove graham cracker crumbs from jar and sprinkle over butter. Pour condensed milk evenly over crumbs. Carefully sprinkle coconut and peanut butter chips in even layers, then cereal, chocolate chips and candies; press gently.

3. Bake 25 to 27 minutes or until top just begins to brown. Cool completely in pan on wire rack. Cut into bars.

Makes about 36 bars

Easy Layered Bars

½ cup (1 stick) butter or margarine, melted

1 can (14 ounces) sweetened condensed milk

1 jar Easy Layered Bar Mix

1. Preheat oven to 350°F. Lightly spray sides of 13×9-inch baking pan with nonstick cooking spray. Pour butter evenly into pan.

2. Remove graham cracker crumbs from jar and sprinkle over butter. Pour condensed milk evenly over crumbs. Carefully sprinkle coconut and peanut butter chips in even layers, then cereal, chocolate chips and candies; press gently.

3. Bake 25 to 27 minutes or until top just begins to brown. Cool completely in pan on wire rack. Cut into bars.

Makes about 36 bars

Easy Layered Bars

½ cup (1 stick) butter or margarine, melted

1 can (14 ounces) sweetened condensed milk

1 jar Easy Layered Bar Mix

1. Preheat oven to 350°F. Lightly spray sides of 13×9-inch baking pan with nonstick cooking spray. Pour butter evenly into pan.

2. Remove graham cracker crumbs from jar and sprinkle over butter. Pour condensed milk evenly over crumbs. Carefully sprinkle coconut and peanut butter chips in even layers, then cereal, chocolate chips and candies; press gently.

3. Bake 25 to 27 minutes or until top just begins to brown. Cool completely in pan on wire rack. Cut into bars.

Makes about 36 bars

Easy Layered Bars

½ cup (1 stick) butter or margarine, melted

1 can (14 ounces) sweetened condensed milk

1 jar Easy Layered Bar Mix

1. Preheat oven to 350°F. Lightly spray sides of 13×9-inch baking pan with nonstick cooking spray. Pour butter evenly into pan.
2. Remove graham cracker crumbs from jar and sprinkle over butter. Pour condensed milk evenly over crumbs. Carefully sprinkle coconut and peanut butter chips in even layers, then cereal, chocolate chips and candies; press gently.
3. Bake 25 to 27 minutes or until top just begins to brown. Cool completely in pan on wire rack. Cut into bars.

Makes about 36 bars

Easy Layered Bars

½ cup (1 stick) butter or margarine, melted

1 can (14 ounces) sweetened condensed milk

1 jar Easy Layered Bar Mix

1. Preheat oven to 350°F. Lightly spray sides of 13×9-inch baking pan with nonstick cooking spray. Pour butter evenly into pan.
2. Remove graham cracker crumbs from jar and sprinkle over butter. Pour condensed milk evenly over crumbs. Carefully sprinkle coconut and peanut butter chips in even layers, then cereal, chocolate chips and candies; press gently.
3. Bake 25 to 27 minutes or until top just begins to brown. Cool completely in pan on wire rack. Cut into bars.

Makes about 36 bars

Easy Layered Bars

½ cup (1 stick) butter or margarine, melted

1 can (14 ounces) sweetened condensed milk

1 jar Easy Layered Bar Mix

1. Preheat oven to 350°F. Lightly spray sides of 13×9-inch baking pan with nonstick cooking spray. Pour butter evenly into pan.
2. Remove graham cracker crumbs from jar and sprinkle over butter. Pour condensed milk evenly over crumbs. Carefully sprinkle coconut and peanut butter chips in even layers, then cereal, chocolate chips and candies; press gently.
3. Bake 25 to 27 minutes or until top just begins to brown. Cool completely in pan on wire rack. Cut into bars.

Makes about 36 bars

Chocolate-Cranberry Pumpkin Pancake Mix

2 cups all-purpose flour
2 teaspoons baking powder
½ teaspoon salt
½ teaspoon ground cinnamon
¼ teaspoon baking soda
¼ teaspoon ground ginger
¼ teaspoon ground nutmeg
⅓ cup packed brown sugar
½ cup bittersweet or semisweet chocolate chips
⅓ cup cinnamon chips
½ cup dried cranberries

Layer ingredients in 1-quart food storage jar with tight-fitting lid in following order: combined flour, baking powder, salt, cinnamon, baking soda, ginger and nutmeg; brown sugar, lightly packed; chocolate chips; cinnamon chips; and cranberries in small plastic bag. Seal jar; cover lid with fabric. Attach gift tag and fabric to jar with raffia. *Makes one 1-quart jar*

Chocolate-Cranberry Pumpkin Pancakes

1 jar Chocolate-Cranberry Pumpkin Pancake Mix
2 eggs
1¼ cups milk
½ cup canned pumpkin
¼ cup vegetable oil
1 teaspoon butter
Maple-flavored syrup (optional)

1. Remove bag of cranberries from jar; set aside. Place remaining contents of jar in large bowl.

2. Beat eggs in medium bowl; stir in milk, pumpkin and oil. Pour egg mixture into jar mixture; stir until just blended. Stir in cranberries.

3. Coat griddle with butter. Heat over medium heat. Pour ¼ cup batter onto griddle for each pancake. Cook until bubbles form and bottoms are brown; turn and cook about 2 minutes or until brown and cooked through. *Makes 16 to 18 (4-inch) pancakes*

Chocolate-Cranberry Pumpkin Pancakes

- 1 jar Chocolate-Cranberry Pumpkin Pancake Mix
- 2 eggs
- 1¼ cups milk
- ½ cup canned pumpkin
- ¼ cup vegetable oil
- 1 teaspoon butter
- Maple-flavored syrup (optional)

1. Remove bag of cranberries from jar; set aside. Place remaining contents of jar in large bowl.
2. Beat eggs in medium bowl; stir in milk, pumpkin and oil. Pour egg mixture into jar mixture; stir until just blended. Stir in cranberries.
3. Coat griddle with butter. Heat over medium heat. Pour ¼ cup batter onto griddle for each pancake. Cook until bubbles form and bottoms are brown; turn and cook about 2 minutes or until brown and cooked through.

Makes 16 to 18 (4-inch) pancakes

Chocolate-Cranberry Pumpkin Pancakes

- 1 jar Chocolate-Cranberry Pumpkin Pancake Mix
- 2 eggs
- 1¼ cups milk
- ½ cup canned pumpkin
- ¼ cup vegetable oil
- 1 teaspoon butter
- Maple-flavored syrup (optional)

1. Remove bag of cranberries from jar; set aside. Place remaining contents of jar in large bowl.
2. Beat eggs in medium bowl; stir in milk, pumpkin and oil. Pour egg mixture into jar mixture; stir until just blended. Stir in cranberries.
3. Coat griddle with butter. Heat over medium heat. Pour ¼ cup batter onto griddle for each pancake. Cook until bubbles form and bottoms are brown; turn and cook about 2 minutes or until brown and cooked through.

Makes 16 to 18 (4-inch) pancakes

Chocolate-Cranberry Pumpkin Pancakes

- 1 jar Chocolate-Cranberry Pumpkin Pancake Mix
- 2 eggs
- 1¼ cups milk
- ½ cup canned pumpkin
- ¼ cup vegetable oil
- 1 teaspoon butter
- Maple-flavored syrup (optional)

1. Remove bag of cranberries from jar; set aside. Place remaining contents of jar in large bowl.
2. Beat eggs in medium bowl; stir in milk, pumpkin and oil. Pour egg mixture into jar mixture; stir until just blended. Stir in cranberries.
3. Coat griddle with butter. Heat over medium heat. Pour ¼ cup batter onto griddle for each pancake. Cook until bubbles form and bottoms are brown; turn and cook about 2 minutes or until brown and cooked through.

Makes 16 to 18 (4-inch) pancakes

Chocolate-Cranberry Pumpkin Pancakes

1 jar Chocolate-Cranberry Pumpkin Pancake Mix
2 eggs
1¼ cups milk
½ cup canned pumpkin
¼ cup vegetable oil
1 teaspoon butter
Maple-flavored syrup (optional)

1. Remove bag of cranberries from jar; set aside. Place remaining contents of jar in large bowl.
2. Beat eggs in medium bowl; stir in milk, pumpkin and oil. Pour egg mixture into jar mixture; stir until just blended. Stir in cranberries.
3. Coat griddle with butter. Heat over medium heat. Pour ¼ cup batter onto griddle for each pancake. Cook until bubbles form and bottoms are brown; turn and cook about 2 minutes or until brown and cooked through.

Makes 16 to 18 (4-inch) pancakes

Chocolate-Cranberry Pumpkin Pancakes

1 jar Chocolate-Cranberry Pumpkin Pancake Mix
2 eggs
1¼ cups milk
½ cup canned pumpkin
¼ cup vegetable oil
1 teaspoon butter
Maple-flavored syrup (optional)

1. Remove bag of cranberries from jar; set aside. Place remaining contents of jar in large bowl.
2. Beat eggs in medium bowl; stir in milk, pumpkin and oil. Pour egg mixture into jar mixture; stir until just blended. Stir in cranberries.
3. Coat griddle with butter. Heat over medium heat. Pour ¼ cup batter onto griddle for each pancake. Cook until bubbles form and bottoms are brown; turn and cook about 2 minutes or until brown and cooked through.

Makes 16 to 18 (4-inch) pancakes

Chocolate-Cranberry Pumpkin Pancakes

1 jar Chocolate-Cranberry Pumpkin Pancake Mix
2 eggs
1¼ cups milk
½ cup canned pumpkin
¼ cup vegetable oil
1 teaspoon butter
Maple-flavored syrup (optional)

1. Remove bag of cranberries from jar; set aside. Place remaining contents of jar in large bowl.
2. Beat eggs in medium bowl; stir in milk, pumpkin and oil. Pour egg mixture into jar mixture; stir until just blended. Stir in cranberries.
3. Coat griddle with butter. Heat over medium heat. Pour ¼ cup batter onto griddle for each pancake. Cook until bubbles form and bottoms are brown; turn and cook about 2 minutes or until brown and cooked through.

Makes 16 to 18 (4-inch) pancakes

Banana Snack Cake Mix

½ cup granulated sugar
¾ cup packed brown sugar
1¼ cups all-purpose flour
1 teaspoon baking powder
¾ teaspoon salt
½ teaspoon baking soda
½ cup chopped walnuts
1 cup semisweet chocolate chips

Layer ingredients in 1-quart food storage jar with tight-fitting lid in following order: granulated sugar; brown sugar, lightly packed; combined flour, baking powder, salt and baking soda; walnuts; and chocolate chips. Seal jar; cover lid with fabric. Attach gift tag and fabric to jar with raffia. *Makes one 1-quart jar*

Banana Snack Cake

1 jar Banana Snack Cake Mix
1¼ cups mashed ripe bananas (about 4 medium)
½ cup vegetable oil
2 eggs, beaten
1 teaspoon vanilla
Chocolate Frosting (optional)

1. Preheat oven to 350°F. Grease and flour 8×8-inch or 9×9-inch baking pan.

2. Place contents of jar in large bowl. Add bananas, oil, eggs and vanilla; stir until well blended. Pour batter into prepared pan.

3. Bake 40 to 45 minutes or until toothpick inserted into center comes out clean. Cool completely in pan on wire rack. Frost, if desired.

Makes 9 to 12 servings

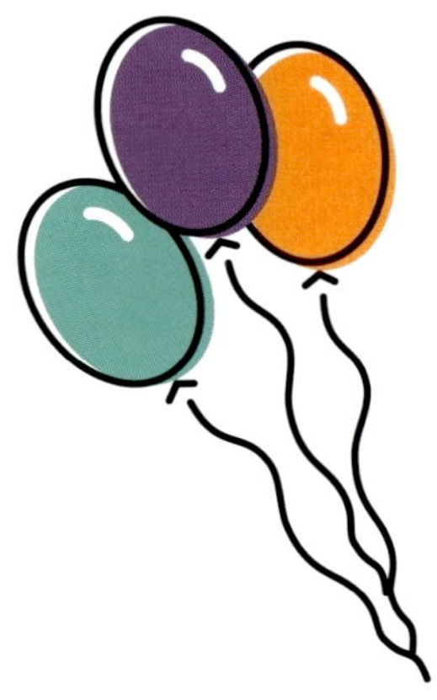

Banana Snack Cake

1 jar Banana Snack Cake Mix
1¼ cups mashed ripe bananas (about 4 medium)
½ cup vegetable oil
2 eggs, beaten
1 teaspoon vanilla
Chocolate frosting (optional)

1. Preheat oven to 350°F. Grease and flour 8×8-inch or 9×9-inch baking pan.
2. Place contents of jar in large bowl. Add bananas, oil, eggs and vanilla; stir until well blended. Pour batter into prepared pan.
3. Bake 40 to 45 minutes or until toothpick inserted into center comes out clean. Cool completely in pan on wire rack. Frost, if desired.

Makes 9 to 12 servings

Banana Snack Cake

1 jar Banana Snack Cake Mix
1¼ cups mashed ripe bananas (about 4 medium)
½ cup vegetable oil
2 eggs, beaten
1 teaspoon vanilla
Chocolate frosting (optional)

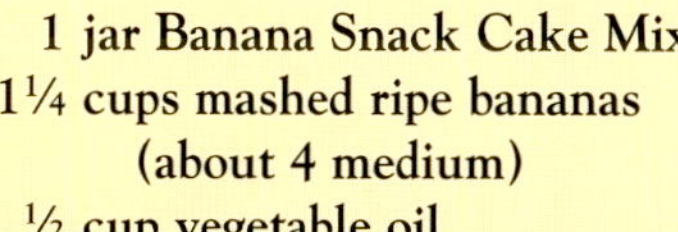

1. Preheat oven to 350°F. Grease and flour 8×8-inch or 9×9-inch baking pan.
2. Place contents of jar in large bowl. Add bananas, oil, eggs and vanilla; stir until well blended. Pour batter into prepared pan.
3. Bake 40 to 45 minutes or until toothpick inserted into center comes out clean. Cool completely in pan on wire rack. Frost, if desired.

Makes 9 to 12 servings

Banana Snack Cake

1 jar Banana Snack Cake Mix
1¼ cups mashed ripe bananas (about 4 medium)
½ cup vegetable oil
2 eggs, beaten
1 teaspoon vanilla
Chocolate frosting (optional)

1. Preheat oven to 350°F. Grease and flour 8×8-inch or 9×9-inch baking pan.
2. Place contents of jar in large bowl. Add bananas, oil, eggs and vanilla; stir until well blended. Pour batter into prepared pan.
3. Bake 40 to 45 minutes or until toothpick inserted into center comes out clean. Cool completely in pan on wire rack. Frost, if desired.

Makes 9 to 12 servings

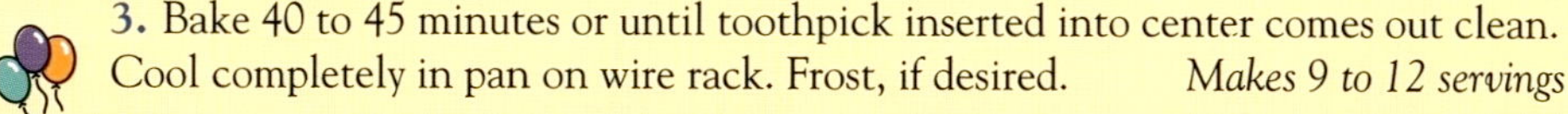

Banana Snack Cake

1 jar Banana Snack Cake Mix
1¼ cups mashed ripe bananas (about 4 medium)
½ cup vegetable oil
2 eggs, beaten
1 teaspoon vanilla
Chocolate frosting (optional)

1. Preheat oven to 350°F. Grease and flour 8×8-inch or 9×9-inch baking pan.
2. Place contents of jar in large bowl. Add bananas, oil, eggs and vanilla; stir until well blended. Pour batter into prepared pan.
3. Bake 40 to 45 minutes or until toothpick inserted into center comes out clean. Cool completely in pan on wire rack. Frost, if desired.

Makes 9 to 12 servings

Banana Snack Cake

1 jar Banana Snack Cake Mix
1¼ cups mashed ripe bananas (about 4 medium)
½ cup vegetable oil
2 eggs, beaten
1 teaspoon vanilla
Chocolate frosting (optional)

1. Preheat oven to 350°F. Grease and flour 8×8-inch or 9×9-inch baking pan.
2. Place contents of jar in large bowl. Add bananas, oil, eggs and vanilla; stir until well blended. Pour batter into prepared pan.
3. Bake 40 to 45 minutes or until toothpick inserted into center comes out clean. Cool completely in pan on wire rack. Frost, if desired.

Makes 9 to 12 servings

Banana Snack Cake

1 jar Banana Snack Cake Mix
1¼ cups mashed ripe bananas (about 4 medium)
½ cup vegetable oil
2 eggs, beaten
1 teaspoon vanilla
Chocolate frosting (optional)

1. Preheat oven to 350°F. Grease and flour 8×8-inch or 9×9-inch baking pan.
2. Place contents of jar in large bowl. Add bananas, oil, eggs and vanilla; stir until well blended. Pour batter into prepared pan.
3. Bake 40 to 45 minutes or until toothpick inserted into center comes out clean. Cool completely in pan on wire rack. Frost, if desired.

Makes 9 to 12 servings

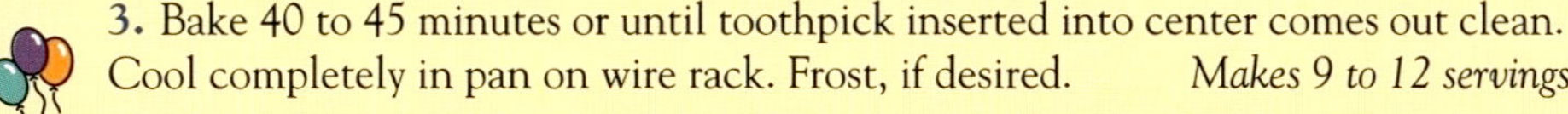

Oatmeal, Coconut & Chip Bar Mix

¼ cup granulated sugar
½ cup packed light brown sugar
1½ cups all-purpose flour
½ teaspoon salt
½ teaspoon baking powder
1½ cups uncooked quick oats
¾ cup flaked coconut
1½ cups semisweet chocolate chips

Layer ingredients in 1½ quart food storage jar with tight-fitting lid in following order: granulated sugar; brown sugar, lightly packed; combined flour, salt and baking powder; oats; coconut; and chocolate chips. Seal jar; cover lid with fabric. Attach gift tag and fabric to jar with raffia. *Makes one 1½-quart jar*

Oatmeal, Coconut & Chip Bars

14 tablespoons (1¾ sticks) butter
1 jar Oatmeal, Coconut & Chip Bar Mix
2 eggs, beaten
1 teaspoon vanilla

1. Preheat oven to 350°F. Grease 13×9-inch baking pan.

2. Place butter in large microwavable bowl. Microwave at HIGH 1 to 1½ minutes or until butter is just melted; cool slightly.

3. Add contents of jar, eggs and vanilla to butter; stir until well blended. Spread batter into prepared pan. Bake 23 to 25 minutes or until edges are slightly brown and center is almost set. Cool completely in pan on wire rack. Cut into bars.

Makes about 3 dozen bars

Oatmeal, Coconut & Chip Bars

14 tablespoons (1¾ sticks) butter
1 jar Oatmeal, Coconut & Chip Bar Mix
2 eggs, beaten
1 teaspoon vanilla

1. Preheat oven to 350°F. Grease 13×9-inch baking pan.
2. Place butter in large microwavable bowl. Microwave at HIGH 1 to 1½ minutes or until butter is just melted; cool slightly.
3. Add contents of jar, eggs and vanilla to butter; stir until well blended. Spread batter into prepared pan. Bake 23 to 25 minutes or until edges are slightly brown and center is almost set. Cool completely in pan on wire rack. Cut into bars.

Makes about 3 dozen bars

Oatmeal, Coconut & Chip Bars

14 tablespoons (1¾ sticks) butter
1 jar Oatmeal, Coconut & Chip Bar Mix
2 eggs, beaten
1 teaspoon vanilla

1. Preheat oven to 350°F. Grease 13×9-inch baking pan.
2. Place butter in large microwavable bowl. Microwave at HIGH 1 to 1½ minutes or until butter is just melted; cool slightly.
3. Add contents of jar, eggs and vanilla to butter; stir until well blended. Spread batter into prepared pan. Bake 23 to 25 minutes or until edges are slightly brown and center is almost set. Cool completely in pan on wire rack. Cut into bars.

Makes about 3 dozen bars

Oatmeal, Coconut & Chip Bars

14 tablespoons (1¾ sticks) butter
1 jar Oatmeal, Coconut & Chip Bar Mix
2 eggs, beaten
1 teaspoon vanilla

1. Preheat oven to 350°F. Grease 13×9-inch baking pan.
2. Place butter in large microwavable bowl. Microwave at HIGH 1 to 1½ minutes or until butter is just melted; cool slightly.
3. Add contents of jar, eggs and vanilla to butter; stir until well blended. Spread batter into prepared pan. Bake 23 to 25 minutes or until edges are slightly brown and center is almost set. Cool completely in pan on wire rack. Cut into bars.

Makes about 3 dozen bars

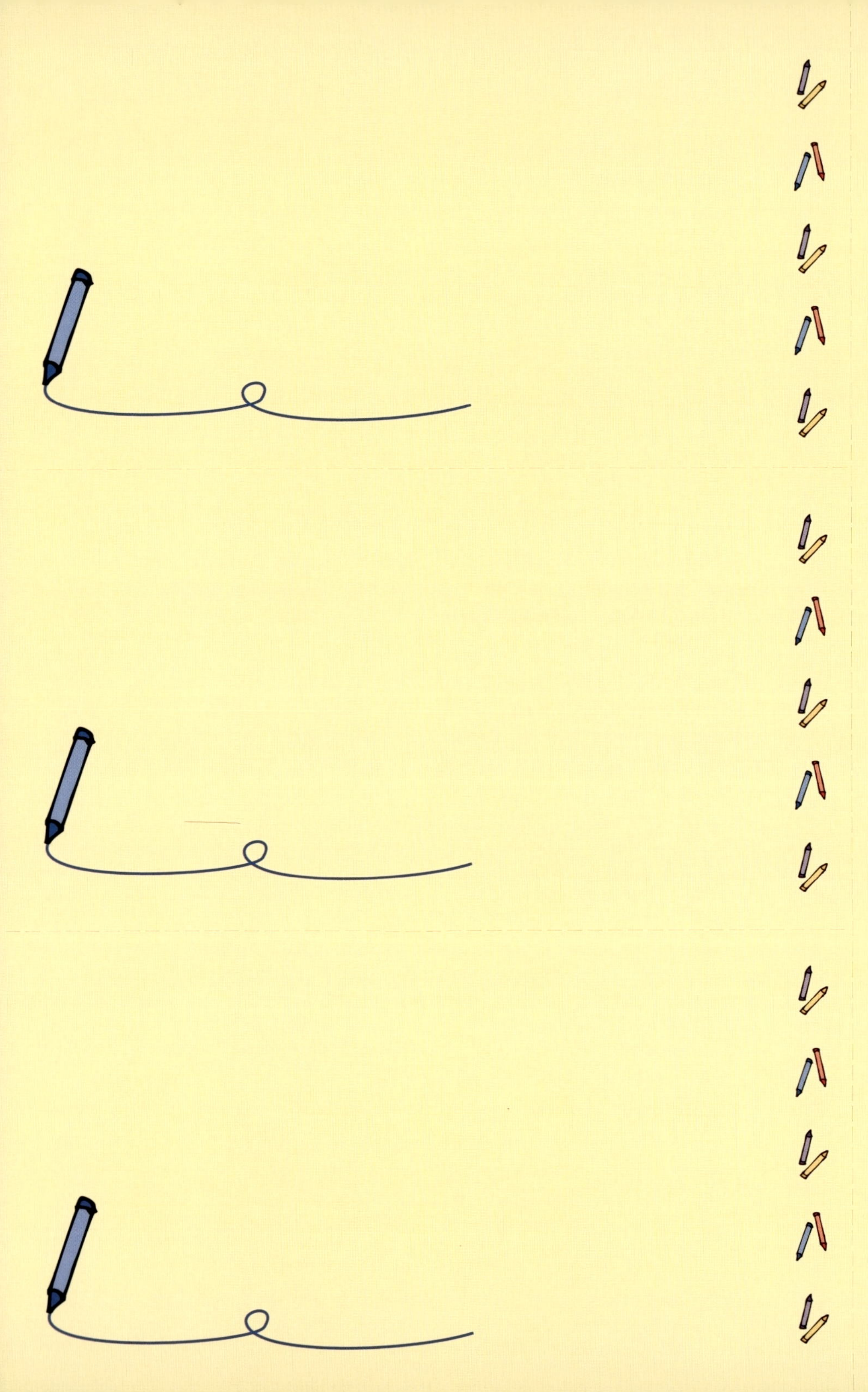

Oatmeal, Coconut & Chip Bars

14 tablespoons (1¾ sticks) butter
1 jar Oatmeal, Coconut & Chip Bar Mix
2 eggs, beaten
1 teaspoon vanilla

1. Preheat oven to 350°F. Grease 13×9-inch baking pan.
2. Place butter in large microwavable bowl. Microwave at HIGH 1 to 1½ minutes or until butter is just melted; cool slightly.
3. Add contents of jar, eggs and vanilla to butter; stir until well blended. Spread batter into prepared pan. Bake 23 to 25 minutes or until edges are slightly brown and center is almost set. Cool completely in pan on wire rack. Cut into bars.

Makes about 3 dozen bars

Oatmeal, Coconut & Chip Bars

14 tablespoons (1¾ sticks) butter
1 jar Oatmeal, Coconut & Chip Bar Mix
2 eggs, beaten
1 teaspoon vanilla

1. Preheat oven to 350°F. Grease 13×9-inch baking pan.
2. Place butter in large microwavable bowl. Microwave at HIGH 1 to 1½ minutes or until butter is just melted; cool slightly.
3. Add contents of jar, eggs and vanilla to butter; stir until well blended. Spread batter into prepared pan. Bake 23 to 25 minutes or until edges are slightly brown and center is almost set. Cool completely in pan on wire rack. Cut into bars.

Makes about 3 dozen bars

Oatmeal, Coconut & Chip Bars

14 tablespoons (1¾ sticks) butter
1 jar Oatmeal, Coconut & Chip Bar Mix
2 eggs, beaten
1 teaspoon vanilla

1. Preheat oven to 350°F. Grease 13×9-inch baking pan.
2. Place butter in large microwavable bowl. Microwave at HIGH 1 to 1½ minutes or until butter is just melted; cool slightly.
3. Add contents of jar, eggs and vanilla to butter; stir until well blended. Spread batter into prepared pan. Bake 23 to 25 minutes or until edges are slightly brown and center is almost set. Cool completely in pan on wire rack. Cut into bars.

Makes about 3 dozen bars

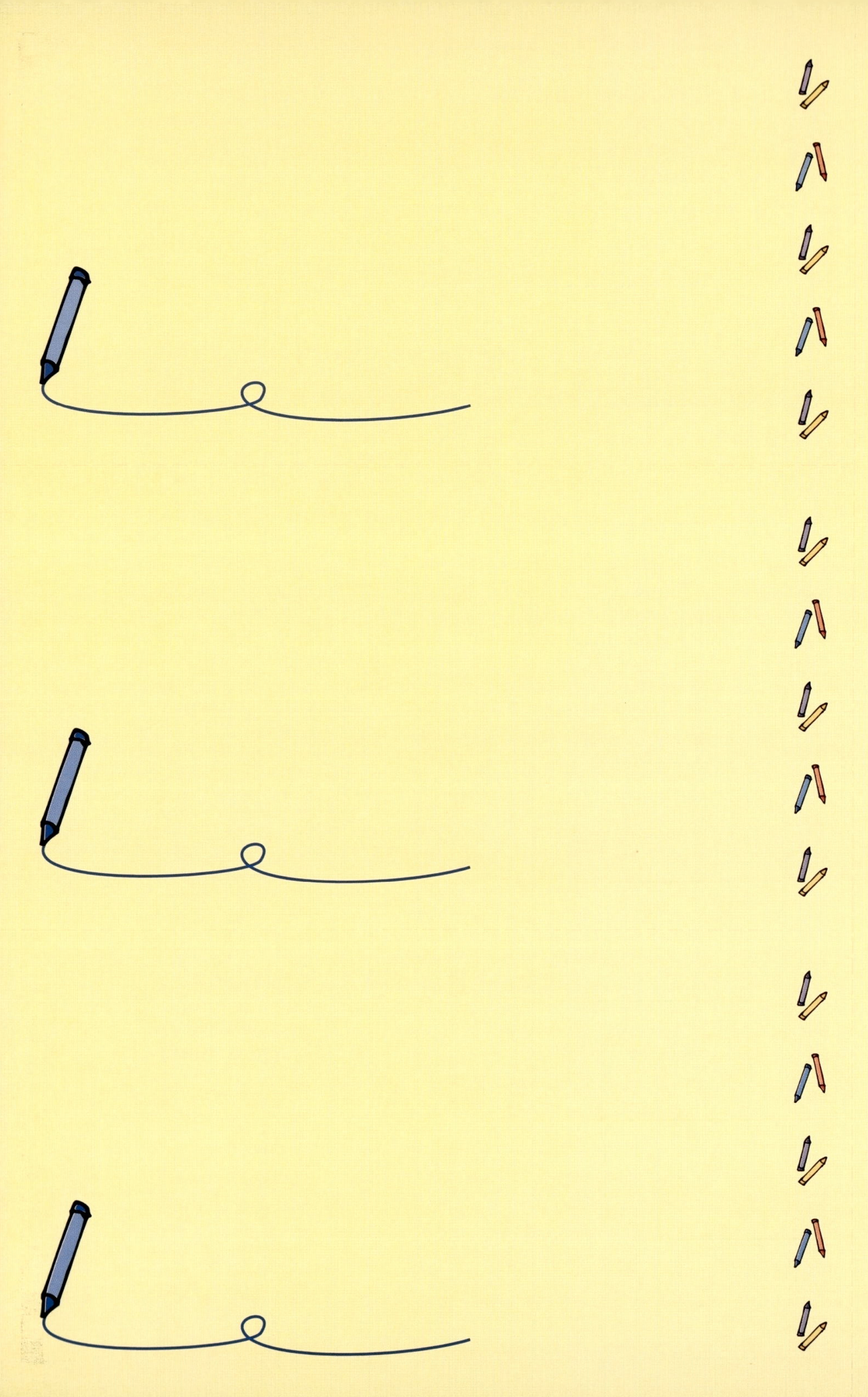

Apple Orchard Pancake Mix

2½ cups all-purpose flour
2 teaspoons baking powder
1¼ teaspoons ground cinnamon
½ teaspoon baking soda
¼ teaspoon salt
¾ cup packed brown sugar
½ cup chopped dried apples
½ cup golden raisins

Layer ingredients in 1-quart food storage jar with tight-fitting lid in following order: combined flour, baking powder, cinnamon, baking soda and salt; brown sugar, lightly packed; apples; and raisins. Seal jar; cover lid with fabric. Attach gift tag and fabric to jar with raffia.

Makes one 1-quart jar

Apple Orchard Pancakes

1 jar Apple Orchard Pancake Mix
2 eggs
1½ cups milk
¼ cup vegetable oil
1 teaspoon butter
Maple-flavored syrup (optional)

1. Place contents of jar in large bowl.

2. Beat eggs in medium bowl; stir in milk and oil. Add egg mixture to jar mix; stir until just blended.

3. Lightly coat griddle with butter. Heat over medium heat until hot. Pour about ¼ cup batter onto griddle for each pancake. Cook until bubbles form and bottom of pancakes are brown; turn and cook about 2 minutes or until brown and cooked through. Serve pancakes with syrup, if desired.

Makes about 20 pancakes

Apple Orchard Pancakes

1 jar Apple Orchard Pancake Mix
2 eggs
1½ cups milk
¼ cup vegetable oil
1 teaspoon butter
Maple-flavored syrup (optional)

1. Place contents of jar in large bowl.
2. Beat eggs in medium bowl; stir in milk and oil. Add egg mixture to jar mix; stir until just blended.
3. Lightly coat griddle with butter. Heat over medium heat until hot. Pour about ¼ cup batter onto griddle for each pancake. Cook until bubbles form and bottom of pancakes are brown; turn and cook about 2 minutes or until brown and cooked through. Serve pancakes with syrup, if desired. *Makes about 20 pancakes*

Apple Orchard Pancakes

1 jar Apple Orchard Pancake Mix
2 eggs
1½ cups milk
¼ cup vegetable oil
1 teaspoon butter
Maple-flavored syrup (optional)

1. Place contents of jar in large bowl.
2. Beat eggs in medium bowl; stir in milk and oil. Add egg mixture to jar mix; stir until just blended.
3. Lightly coat griddle with butter. Heat over medium heat until hot. Pour about ¼ cup batter onto griddle for each pancake. Cook until bubbles form and bottom of pancakes are brown; turn and cook about 2 minutes or until brown and cooked through. Serve pancakes with syrup, if desired. *Makes about 20 pancakes*

Apple Orchard Pancakes

1 jar Apple Orchard Pancake Mix
2 eggs
1½ cups milk
¼ cup vegetable oil
1 teaspoon butter
Maple-flavored syrup (optional)

1. Place contents of jar in large bowl.
2. Beat eggs in medium bowl; stir in milk and oil. Add egg mixture to jar mix; stir until just blended.
3. Lightly coat griddle with butter. Heat over medium heat until hot. Pour about ¼ cup batter onto griddle for each pancake. Cook until bubbles form and bottom of pancakes are brown; turn and cook about 2 minutes or until brown and cooked through. Serve pancakes with syrup, if desired. *Makes about 20 pancakes*

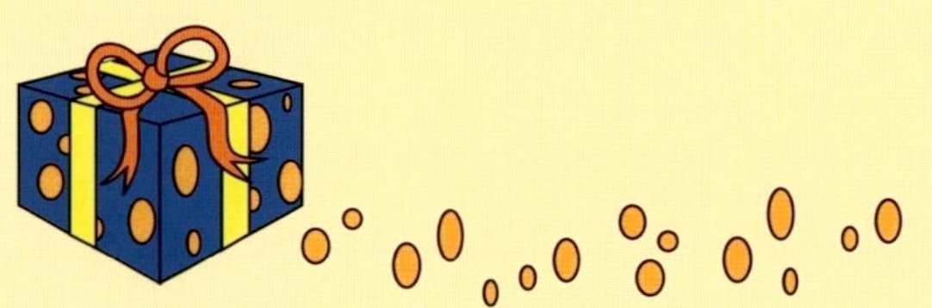

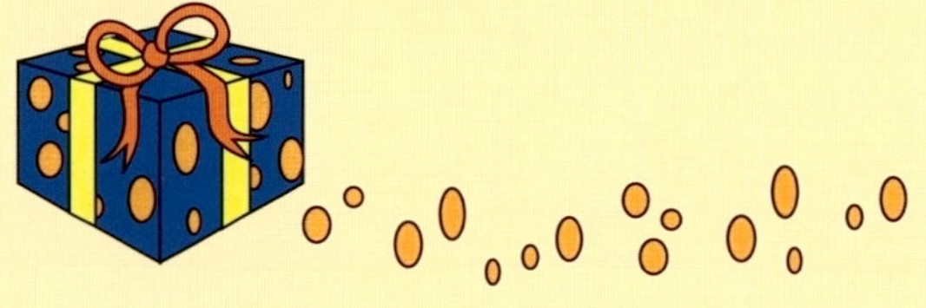

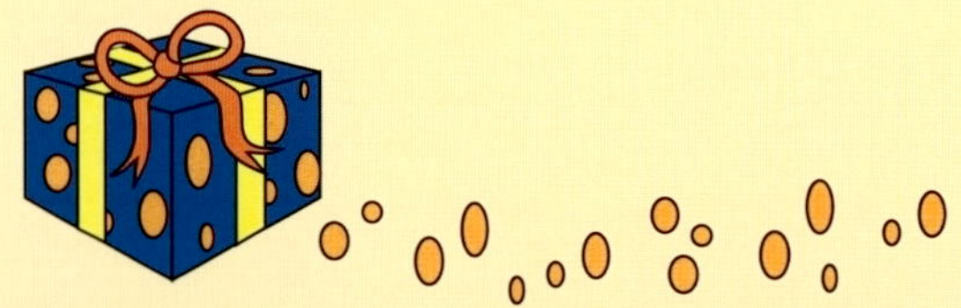

Apple Orchard Pancakes

1 jar Apple Orchard Pancake Mix
2 eggs
1½ cups milk
¼ cup vegetable oil
1 teaspoon butter
Maple-flavored syrup (optional)

1. Place contents of jar in large bowl.
2. Beat eggs in medium bowl; stir in milk and oil. Add egg mixture to jar mix; stir until just blended.
3. Lightly coat griddle with butter. Heat over medium heat until hot. Pour about ¼ cup batter onto griddle for each pancake. Cook until bubbles form and bottom of pancakes are brown; turn and cook about 2 minutes or until brown and cooked through. Serve pancakes with syrup, if desired.

Makes about 20 pancakes

Apple Orchard Pancakes

1 jar Apple Orchard Pancake Mix
2 eggs
1½ cups milk
¼ cup vegetable oil
1 teaspoon butter
Maple-flavored syrup (optional)

1. Place contents of jar in large bowl.
2. Beat eggs in medium bowl; stir in milk and oil. Add egg mixture to jar mix; stir until just blended.
3. Lightly coat griddle with butter. Heat over medium heat until hot. Pour about ¼ cup batter onto griddle for each pancake. Cook until bubbles form and bottom of pancakes are brown; turn and cook about 2 minutes or until brown and cooked through. Serve pancakes with syrup, if desired.

Makes about 20 pancakes

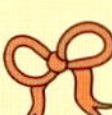

Apple Orchard Pancakes

1 jar Apple Orchard Pancake Mix
2 eggs
1½ cups milk
¼ cup vegetable oil
1 teaspoon butter
Maple-flavored syrup (optional)

1. Place contents of jar in large bowl.
2. Beat eggs in medium bowl; stir in milk and oil. Add egg mixture to jar mix; stir until just blended.
3. Lightly coat griddle with butter. Heat over medium heat until hot. Pour about ¼ cup batter onto griddle for each pancake. Cook until bubbles form and bottom of pancakes are brown; turn and cook about 2 minutes or until brown and cooked through. Serve pancakes with syrup, if desired.

Makes about 20 pancakes

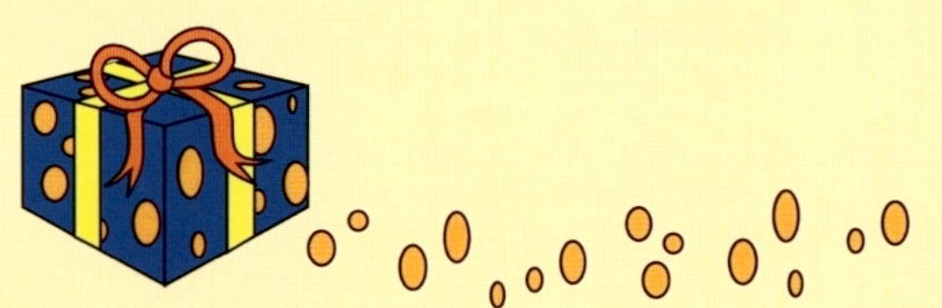

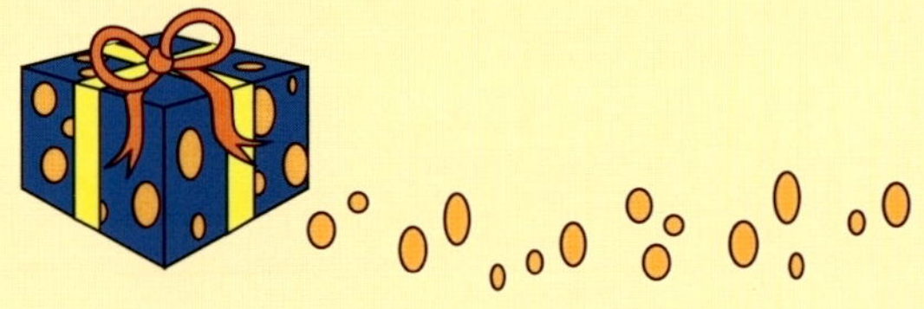

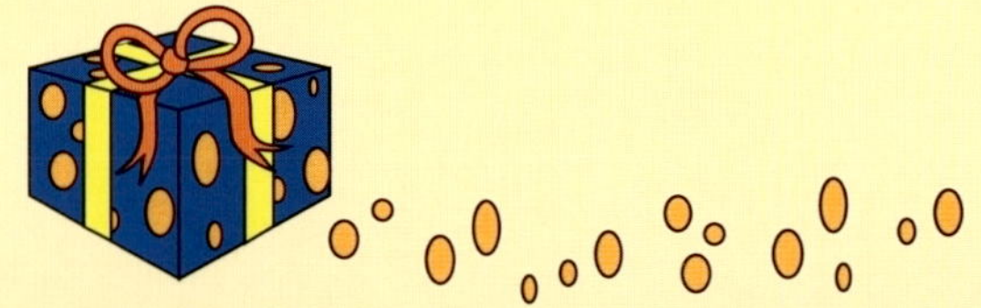

Raisin-Coconut Cookie Mix

½ cup granulated sugar
½ cup packed brown sugar
1¾ cups all-purpose flour
2 teaspoons baking powder
½ teaspoon salt
1¼ cups raisins
2 cups flaked coconut

Layer ingredients in 1½-quart food storage jar with tight-fitting lid in following order: granulated sugar; brown sugar, lightly packed; combined flour, baking powder and salt; raisins; and coconut. Seal jar; cover lid with fabric. Attach gift tag and fabric to jar with raffia.

Makes one 1½-quart jar

Raisin-Coconut Cookies

1 cup (2 sticks) butter, softened
1 egg
1 teaspoon vanilla
1 jar Raisin-Coconut Cookie mix

1. Preheat oven to 350°F.

2. Beat butter 1 minute in large bowl with electric mixer at medium speed. Add egg and vanilla; beat 1 minute. Add contents of jar; beat 2 minutes at low speed or until well blended.

3. Drop dough by rounded teaspoonfuls 2 inches apart onto *ungreased* cookie sheets. Bake 14 to 15 minutes or until set and just beginning to brown around edges. Cool on cookie sheets 2 minutes; remove to wire racks to cool completely.

Makes about 4 dozen cookies

Raisin-Coconut Cookies

1 cup (2 sticks) butter, softened
1 egg
1 teaspoon vanilla
1 jar Raisin-Coconut Cookie mix

1. Preheat oven to 350°F.
2. Beat butter 1 minute in large bowl with electric mixer at medium speed. Add egg and vanilla; beat 1 minute. Add contents of jar; beat 2 minutes at low speed or until well blended.
3. Drop dough by rounded teaspoonfuls 2 inches apart onto *ungreased* cookie sheets. Bake 14 to 15 minutes or until set and just beginning to brown around edges. Cool on cookie sheets 2 minutes; remove to wire racks to cool completely.

Makes about 4 dozen cookies

Raisin-Coconut Cookies

1 cup (2 sticks) butter, softened
1 egg
1 teaspoon vanilla
1 jar Raisin-Coconut Cookie mix

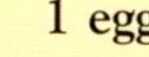

1. Preheat oven to 350°F.
2. Beat butter 1 minute in large bowl with electric mixer at medium speed. Add egg and vanilla; beat 1 minute. Add contents of jar; beat 2 minutes at low speed or until well blended.
3. Drop dough by rounded teaspoonfuls 2 inches apart onto *ungreased* cookie sheets. Bake 14 to 15 minutes or until set and just beginning to brown around edges. Cool on cookie sheets 2 minutes; remove to wire racks to cool completely.

Makes about 4 dozen cookies

Raisin-Coconut Cookies

1 cup (2 sticks) butter, softened
1 egg
1 teaspoon vanilla
1 jar Raisin-Coconut Cookie mix

1. Preheat oven to 350°F.
2. Beat butter 1 minute in large bowl with electric mixer at medium speed. Add egg and vanilla; beat 1 minute. Add contents of jar; beat 2 minutes at low speed or until well blended.
3. Drop dough by rounded teaspoonfuls 2 inches apart onto *ungreased* cookie sheets. Bake 14 to 15 minutes or until set and just beginning to brown around edges. Cool on cookie sheets 2 minutes; remove to wire racks to cool completely.

Makes about 4 dozen cookies

Raisin-Coconut Cookies

1 cup (2 sticks) butter, softened
1 egg
1 teaspoon vanilla
1 jar Raisin-Coconut Cookie mix

1. Preheat oven to 350°F.
2. Beat butter 1 minute in large bowl with electric mixer at medium speed. Add egg and vanilla; beat 1 minute. Add contents of jar; beat 2 minutes at low speed or until well blended.
3. Drop dough by rounded teaspoonfuls 2 inches apart onto *ungreased* cookie sheets. Bake 14 to 15 minutes or until set and just beginning to brown around edges. Cool on cookie sheets 2 minutes; remove to wire racks to cool completely.

Makes about 4 dozen cookies

Raisin-Coconut Cookies

1 cup (2 sticks) butter, softened
1 egg
1 teaspoon vanilla
1 jar Raisin-Coconut Cookie mix

1. Preheat oven to 350°F.
2. Beat butter 1 minute in large bowl with electric mixer at medium speed. Add egg and vanilla; beat 1 minute. Add contents of jar; beat 2 minutes at low speed or until well blended.
3. Drop dough by rounded teaspoonfuls 2 inches apart onto *ungreased* cookie sheets. Bake 14 to 15 minutes or until set and just beginning to brown around edges. Cool on cookie sheets 2 minutes; remove to wire racks to cool completely.

Makes about 4 dozen cookies

Raisin-Coconut Cookies

1 cup (2 sticks) butter, softened
1 egg
1 teaspoon vanilla
1 jar Raisin-Coconut Cookie mix

1. Preheat oven to 350°F.
2. Beat butter 1 minute in large bowl with electric mixer at medium speed. Add egg and vanilla; beat 1 minute. Add contents of jar; beat 2 minutes at low speed or until well blended.
3. Drop dough by rounded teaspoonfuls 2 inches apart onto *ungreased* cookie sheets. Bake 14 to 15 minutes or until set and just beginning to brown around edges. Cool on cookie sheets 2 minutes; remove to wire racks to cool completely.

Makes about 4 dozen cookies

Carrot Snack Cake Mix

½ cup granulated sugar
¾ cup packed brown sugar
1⅓ cups all-purpose flour
1 teaspoon baking powder
1 teaspoon ground cinnamon
½ teaspoon salt
½ teaspoon ground nutmeg
¼ teaspoon baking soda
¼ teaspoon ground allspice
⅔ cup raisins
⅔ cup chopped walnuts or flaked coconut

Layer ingredients in 1-quart food storage jar with tight-fitting lid in following order: granulated sugar; brown sugar, lightly packed; combined flour, baking powder, cinnamon, salt, baking soda, nutmeg and allspice; raisins; and walnuts in small plastic bag. Seal jar; cover lid with fabric. Attach gift tag and fabric to jar with raffia.

Makes one 1-quart jar

Gift Idea: Assemble a gift basket with a jar of Carrot Snack Cake Mix, a container of cream cheese frosting and carrot-shaped candy to decorate cake. Complete the basket with small colorful paper plates and napkins.

Carrot Snack Cake

1 jar Carrot Snack Cake Mix
1 cup vegetable oil
3 eggs
1 teaspoon vanilla
2 cups shredded carrots
1 container cream cheese frosting (optional)

1. Preheat oven to 350°F. Grease 9×9-inch baking pan; set aside.

2. Remove bag of walnuts from jar; set aside. Place remaining contents of jar in large bowl; add oil, eggs and vanilla. Beat 30 seconds with electric mixer at low speed. Beat 1½ minutes on medium speed or until well blended. Stir in carrots and walnuts.

3. Spread batter evenly in prepared pan. Bake 40 to 45 minutes or until toothpick inserted into center comes out clean. Cool completely in pan on wire rack. Frost, if desired.

Makes 20 to 24 servings

Carrot Snack Cake

1 jar Carrot Snack Cake Mix
1 cup vegetable oil
3 eggs
1 teaspoon vanilla
2 cups shredded carrots
1 container cream cheese frosting (optional)

1. Preheat oven to 350°F. Grease 9×9-inch baking pan; set aside.
2. Remove bag of walnuts from jar; set aside. Place remaining contents of jar in large bowl; add oil, eggs and vanilla. Beat 30 seconds with electric mixer at low speed. Beat 1½ minutes on medium speed or until well blended. Stir in carrots and walnuts.
3. Spread batter evenly in prepared pan. Bake 40 to 45 minutes or until toothpick inserted into center comes out clean. Cool completely in pan on wire rack. Spread frost, if desired.

Makes 20 to 24 servings

Carrot Snack Cake

1 jar Carrot Snack Cake Mix
1 cup vegetable oil
3 eggs
1 teaspoon vanilla
2 cups shredded carrots
1 container cream cheese frosting (optional)

1. Preheat oven to 350°F. Grease 9×9-inch baking pan; set aside.
2. Remove bag of walnuts from jar; set aside. Place remaining contents of jar in large bowl; add oil, eggs and vanilla. Beat 30 seconds with electric mixer at low speed. Beat 1½ minutes on medium speed or until well blended. Stir in carrots and walnuts.
3. Spread batter evenly in prepared pan. Bake 40 to 45 minutes or until toothpick inserted into center comes out clean. Cool completely in pan on wire rack. Spread frost, if desired.

Makes 20 to 24 servings

Carrot Snack Cake

1 jar Carrot Snack Cake Mix
1 cup vegetable oil
3 eggs
1 teaspoon vanilla
2 cups shredded carrots
1 container cream cheese frosting (optional)

1. Preheat oven to 350°F. Grease 9×9-inch baking pan; set aside.
2. Remove bag of walnuts from jar; set aside. Place remaining contents of jar in large bowl; add oil, eggs and vanilla. Beat 30 seconds with electric mixer at low speed. Beat 1½ minutes on medium speed or until well blended. Stir in carrots and walnuts.
3. Spread batter evenly in prepared pan. Bake 40 to 45 minutes or until toothpick inserted into center comes out clean. Cool completely in pan on wire rack. Spread frost, if desired.

Makes 20 to 24 servings

Carrot Snack Cake

- 1 jar Carrot Snack Cake Mix
- 1 cup vegetable oil
- 3 eggs
- 1 teaspoon vanilla
- 2 cups shredded carrots
- 1 container cream cheese frosting (optional)

1. Preheat oven to 350°F. Grease 9×9-inch baking pan; set aside.
2. Remove bag of walnuts from jar; set aside. Place remaining contents of jar in large bowl; add oil, eggs and vanilla. Beat 30 seconds with electric mixer at low speed. Beat 1½ minutes on medium speed or until well blended. Stir in carrots and walnuts.
3. Spread batter evenly in prepared pan. Bake 40 to 45 minutes or until toothpick inserted into center comes out clean. Cool completely in pan on wire rack. Spread frost, if desired.

Makes 20 to 24 servings

Carrot Snack Cake

- 1 jar Carrot Snack Cake Mix
- 1 cup vegetable oil
- 3 eggs
- 1 teaspoon vanilla
- 2 cups shredded carrots
- 1 container cream cheese frosting (optional)

1. Preheat oven to 350°F. Grease 9×9-inch baking pan; set aside.
2. Remove bag of walnuts from jar; set aside. Place remaining contents of jar in large bowl; add oil, eggs and vanilla. Beat 30 seconds with electric mixer at low speed. Beat 1½ minutes on medium speed or until well blended. Stir in carrots and walnuts.
3. Spread batter evenly in prepared pan. Bake 40 to 45 minutes or until toothpick inserted into center comes out clean. Cool completely in pan on wire rack. Spread frost, if desired.

Makes 20 to 24 servings

Carrot Snack Cake

- 1 jar Carrot Snack Cake Mix
- 1 cup vegetable oil
- 3 eggs
- 1 teaspoon vanilla
- 2 cups shredded carrots
- 1 container cream cheese frosting (optional)

1. Preheat oven to 350°F. Grease 9×9-inch baking pan; set aside.
2. Remove bag of walnuts from jar; set aside. Place remaining contents of jar in large bowl; add oil, eggs and vanilla. Beat 30 seconds with electric mixer at low speed. Beat 1½ minutes on medium speed or until well blended. Stir in carrots and walnuts.
3. Spread batter evenly in prepared pan. Bake 40 to 45 minutes or until toothpick inserted into center comes out clean. Cool completely in pan on wire rack. Spread frost, if desired.

Makes 20 to 24 servings

Bear Bite Snack Mix

1½ cups sweetened corn and oat cereal
1 cup teddy bear-shaped cookies
½ cup dried fruit bits or chopped mixed dried fruit
1 cup raisins

Layer ingredients in 1-quart food storage jar with tight-fitting lid in following order: cereal; cookies; fruit; and raisins in small plastic bag. Seal jar; cover lid with fabric. Attach gift tag and fabric to jar with raffia.

Makes one 1-quart jar

Bear Bite Snack Mix

2 teaspoons sugar
¾ teaspoon ground cinnamon
¼ teaspoon ground nutmeg
1 jar Bear Bite Snack Mix
Nonstick cooking spray

1. Preheat oven to 350°F. Combine sugar, cinnamon and nutmeg in small bowl; mix well.

2. Remove bag of raisins from jar; set aside. Place remaining contents of jar on jelly-roll pan. Generously spray with cooking spray. Sprinkle with half of sugar mixture. Stir well. Spray again with cooking spray; sprinkle with remaining sugar mixture.

3. Bake 5 minutes; stir in raisins. Bake 5 minutes more; stir. Cool completely in pan on wire rack. Store in air-tight container.

Makes 4 cups snack mix

Bear Bite Snack Mix

2 teaspoons sugar
¾ teaspoon ground cinnamon
¼ teaspoon ground nutmeg
1 jar Bear Bite Snack Mix
Nonstick cooking spray

1. Preheat oven to 350°F. Combine sugar, cinnamon and nutmeg in small bowl; mix well.
2. Remove bag of raisins from jar; set aside. Place remaining contents of jar on jelly-roll pan. Generously spray with cooking spray. Sprinkle with half of sugar mixture. Stir well. Spray again with cooking spray; sprinkle with remaining sugar mixture.
3. Bake 5 minutes; stir in raisins. Bake 5 minutes more; stir. Cool completely in pan on wire rack. Store in air-tight container. *Makes 4 cups snack mix*

Bear Bite Snack Mix

2 teaspoons sugar
¾ teaspoon ground cinnamon
¼ teaspoon ground nutmeg
1 jar Bear Bite Snack Mix
Nonstick cooking spray

1. Preheat oven to 350°F. Combine sugar, cinnamon and nutmeg in small bowl; mix well.
2. Remove bag of raisins from jar; set aside. Place remaining contents of jar on jelly-roll pan. Generously spray with cooking spray. Sprinkle with half of sugar mixture. Stir well. Spray again with cooking spray; sprinkle with remaining sugar mixture.
3. Bake 5 minutes; stir in raisins. Bake 5 minutes more; stir. Cool completely in pan on wire rack. Store in air-tight container. *Makes 4 cups snack mix*

Bear Bite Snack Mix

2 teaspoons sugar
¾ teaspoon ground cinnamon
¼ teaspoon ground nutmeg
1 jar Bear Bite Snack Mix
Nonstick cooking spray

1. Preheat oven to 350°F. Combine sugar, cinnamon and nutmeg in small bowl; mix well.
2. Remove bag of raisins from jar; set aside. Place remaining contents of jar on jelly-roll pan. Generously spray with cooking spray. Sprinkle with half of sugar mixture. Stir well. Spray again with cooking spray; sprinkle with remaining sugar mixture.
3. Bake 5 minutes; stir in raisins. Bake 5 minutes more; stir. Cool completely in pan on wire rack. Store in air-tight container. *Makes 4 cups snack mix*

Bear Bite Snack Mix

2 teaspoons sugar
¾ teaspoon ground cinnamon
¼ teaspoon ground nutmeg
1 jar Bear Bite Snack Mix
Nonstick cooking spray

1. Preheat oven to 350°F. Combine sugar, cinnamon and nutmeg in small bowl; mix well.
2. Remove bag of raisins from jar; set aside. Place remaining contents of jar on jelly-roll pan. Generously spray with cooking spray. Sprinkle with half of sugar mixture. Stir well. Spray again with cooking spray; sprinkle with remaining sugar mixture.
3. Bake 5 minutes; stir in raisins. Bake 5 minutes more; stir. Cool completely in pan on wire rack. Store in air-tight container.

Makes 4 cups snack mix

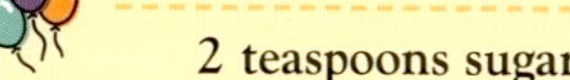

Bear Bite Snack Mix

2 teaspoons sugar
¾ teaspoon ground cinnamon
¼ teaspoon ground nutmeg
1 jar Bear Bite Snack Mix
Nonstick cooking spray

1. Preheat oven to 350°F. Combine sugar, cinnamon and nutmeg in small bowl; mix well.
2. Remove bag of raisins from jar; set aside. Place remaining contents of jar on jelly-roll pan. Generously spray with cooking spray. Sprinkle with half of sugar mixture. Stir well. Spray again with cooking spray; sprinkle with remaining sugar mixture.
3. Bake 5 minutes; stir in raisins. Bake 5 minutes more; stir. Cool completely in pan on wire rack. Store in air-tight container.

Makes 4 cups snack mix

Bear Bite Snack Mix

2 teaspoons sugar
¾ teaspoon ground cinnamon
¼ teaspoon ground nutmeg
1 jar Bear Bite Snack Mix
Nonstick cooking spray

1. Preheat oven to 350°F. Combine sugar, cinnamon and nutmeg in small bowl; mix well.
2. Remove bag of raisins from jar; set aside. Place remaining contents of jar on jelly-roll pan. Generously spray with cooking spray. Sprinkle with half of sugar mixture. Stir well. Spray again with cooking spray; sprinkle with remaining sugar mixture.
3. Bake 5 minutes; stir in raisins. Bake 5 minutes more; stir. Cool completely in pan on wire rack. Store in air-tight container.

Makes 4 cups snack mix

Apple-Cinnamon Chip Muffin Mix

½ cup whole wheat flour
1 cup all-purpose flour
1 teaspoon baking powder
¼ teaspoon ground nutmeg
¼ teaspoon salt
⅔ cup packed brown sugar
⅔ cup cinnamon chips
½ cup seedless raisins
½ cup chopped dried apples

Layer ingredients in 1-quart food storage jar with tight-fitting lid in following order: whole wheat flour; combined flour, baking powder, nutmeg and salt; brown sugar, lightly packed; cinnamon chips; raisins; and dried apples in small plastic bag. Seal jar; cover lid with fabric. Attach label and fabric to jar with raffia.

Makes one 1-quart jar

Gift Idea: Assemble a gift basket with a jar of Apple-Cinnamon Chip Muffin Mix, a jar of applesauce, paper or foil muffin cup liners and a container of whipped butter. Complete the basket with colorful cloth or paper napkins.

Apple-Cinnamon Chip Muffins

1 jar Apple-Cinnamon Chip Muffin Mix
⅔ cup unsweetened applesauce
2 eggs, beaten
⅓ cup vegetable oil
2 tablespoons apple juice or water

1. Preheat oven to 400°F. Line 12 (2¾-inch) muffin cups with paper or foil baking cups.

2. Remove bag of dried apples from jar. Place remaining contents of jar in large bowl; stir in dried apples, separating pieces with fingers, if necessary.

3. Combine applesauce, eggs, oil and apple juice in medium bowl. Add to contents of jar; stir until just blended. Fill muffin cups ⅔ to ¾ full with batter. Bake 15 to 17 minutes or until toothpick inserted into centers comes out clean. Cool on wire rack. Serve warm or at room temperature.

Makes 12 muffins

Apple-Cinnamon Chip Muffins

1 jar Apple-Cinnamon Chip Muffin Mix
⅔ cup unsweetened applesauce
2 eggs, beaten
⅓ cup vegetable oil
2 tablespoons apple juice or water

1. Preheat oven to 400°F. Line 12 (2¾-inch) muffin cups with paper or foil baking cups.
2. Remove bag of dried apples from jar. Place remaining contents of jar in large bowl; stir in dried apples, separating pieces with fingers, if necessary.
3. Combine applesauce, eggs, oil and apple juice in medium bowl. Add to contents of jar; stir until just blended. Fill muffin cups ⅔ to ¾ full with batter. Bake 15 to 17 minutes or until toothpick inserted into centers comes out clean. Cool on wire rack. Serve warm or at room temperature. *Makes 12 muffins*

Apple-Cinnamon Chip Muffins

1 jar Apple-Cinnamon Chip Muffin Mix
⅔ cup unsweetened applesauce
2 eggs, beaten
⅓ cup vegetable oil
2 tablespoons apple juice or water

1. Preheat oven to 400°F. Line 12 (2¾-inch) muffin cups with paper or foil baking cups.
2. Remove bag of dried apples from jar. Place remaining contents of jar in large bowl; stir in dried apples, separating pieces with fingers, if necessary.
3. Combine applesauce, eggs, oil and apple juice in medium bowl. Add to contents of jar; stir until just blended. Fill muffin cups ⅔ to ¾ full with batter. Bake 15 to 17 minutes or until toothpick inserted into centers comes out clean. Cool on wire rack. Serve warm or at room temperature. *Makes 12 muffins*

Apple-Cinnamon Chip Muffins

1 jar Apple-Cinnamon Chip Muffin Mix
⅔ cup unsweetened applesauce
2 eggs, beaten
⅓ cup vegetable oil
2 tablespoons apple juice or water

1. Preheat oven to 400°F. Line 12 (2¾-inch) muffin cups with paper or foil baking cups.
2. Remove bag of dried apples from jar. Place remaining contents of jar in large bowl; stir in dried apples, separating pieces with fingers, if necessary.
3. Combine applesauce, eggs, oil and apple juice in medium bowl. Add to contents of jar; stir until just blended. Fill muffin cups ⅔ to ¾ full with batter. Bake 15 to 17 minutes or until toothpick inserted into centers comes out clean. Cool on wire rack. Serve warm or at room temperature. *Makes 12 muffins*

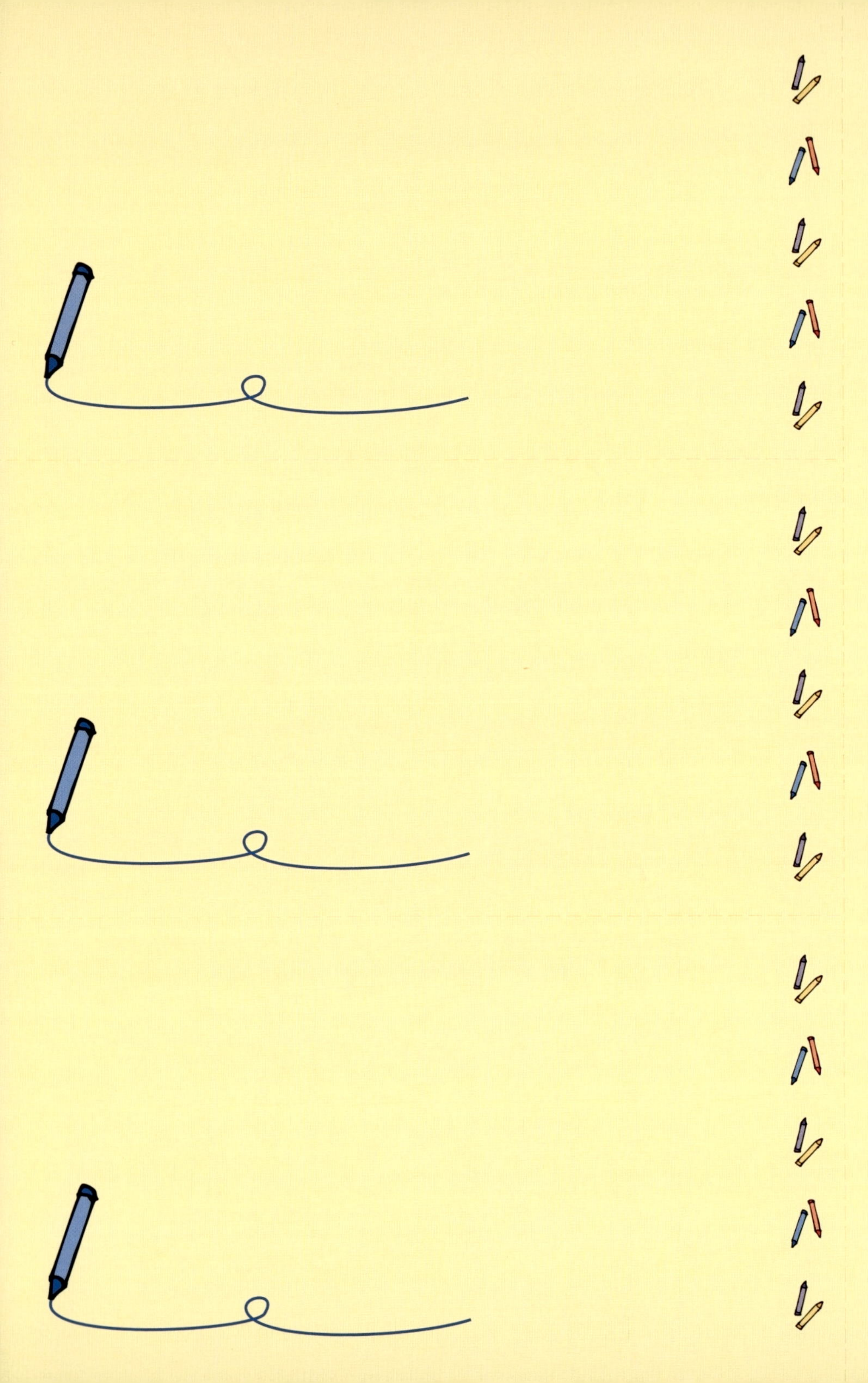

Apple-Cinnamon Chip Muffins

1 jar Apple-Cinnamon Chip Muffin Mix
⅔ cup unsweetened applesauce
2 eggs, beaten
⅓ cup vegetable oil
2 tablespoons apple juice or water

1. Preheat oven to 400°F. Line 12 (2¾-inch) muffin cups with paper or foil baking cups.
2. Remove bag of dried apples from jar. Place remaining contents of jar in large bowl; stir in dried apples, separating pieces with fingers, if necessary.
3. Combine applesauce, eggs, oil and apple juice in medium bowl. Add to contents of jar; stir until just blended. Fill muffin cups ⅔ to ¾ full with batter. Bake 15 to 17 minutes or until toothpick inserted into centers comes out clean. Cool on wire rack. Serve warm or at room temperature. *Makes 12 muffins*

Apple-Cinnamon Chip Muffins

1 jar Apple-Cinnamon Chip Muffin Mix
⅔ cup unsweetened applesauce
2 eggs, beaten
⅓ cup vegetable oil
2 tablespoons apple juice or water

1. Preheat oven to 400°F. Line 12 (2¾-inch) muffin cups with paper or foil baking cups.
2. Remove bag of dried apples from jar. Place remaining contents of jar in large bowl; stir in dried apples, separating pieces with fingers, if necessary.
3. Combine applesauce, eggs, oil and apple juice in medium bowl. Add to contents of jar; stir until just blended. Fill muffin cups ⅔ to ¾ full with batter. Bake 15 to 17 minutes or until toothpick inserted into centers comes out clean. Cool on wire rack. Serve warm or at room temperature. *Makes 12 muffins*

Apple-Cinnamon Chip Muffins

1 jar Apple-Cinnamon Chip Muffin Mix
⅔ cup unsweetened applesauce
2 eggs, beaten
⅓ cup vegetable oil
2 tablespoons apple juice or water

1. Preheat oven to 400°F. Line 12 (2¾-inch) muffin cups with paper or foil baking cups.
2. Remove bag of dried apples from jar. Place remaining contents of jar in large bowl; stir in dried apples, separating pieces with fingers, if necessary.
3. Combine applesauce, eggs, oil and apple juice in medium bowl. Add to contents of jar; stir until just blended. Fill muffin cups ⅔ to ¾ full with batter. Bake 15 to 17 minutes or until toothpick inserted into centers comes out clean. Cool on wire rack. Serve warm or at room temperature. *Makes 12 muffins*

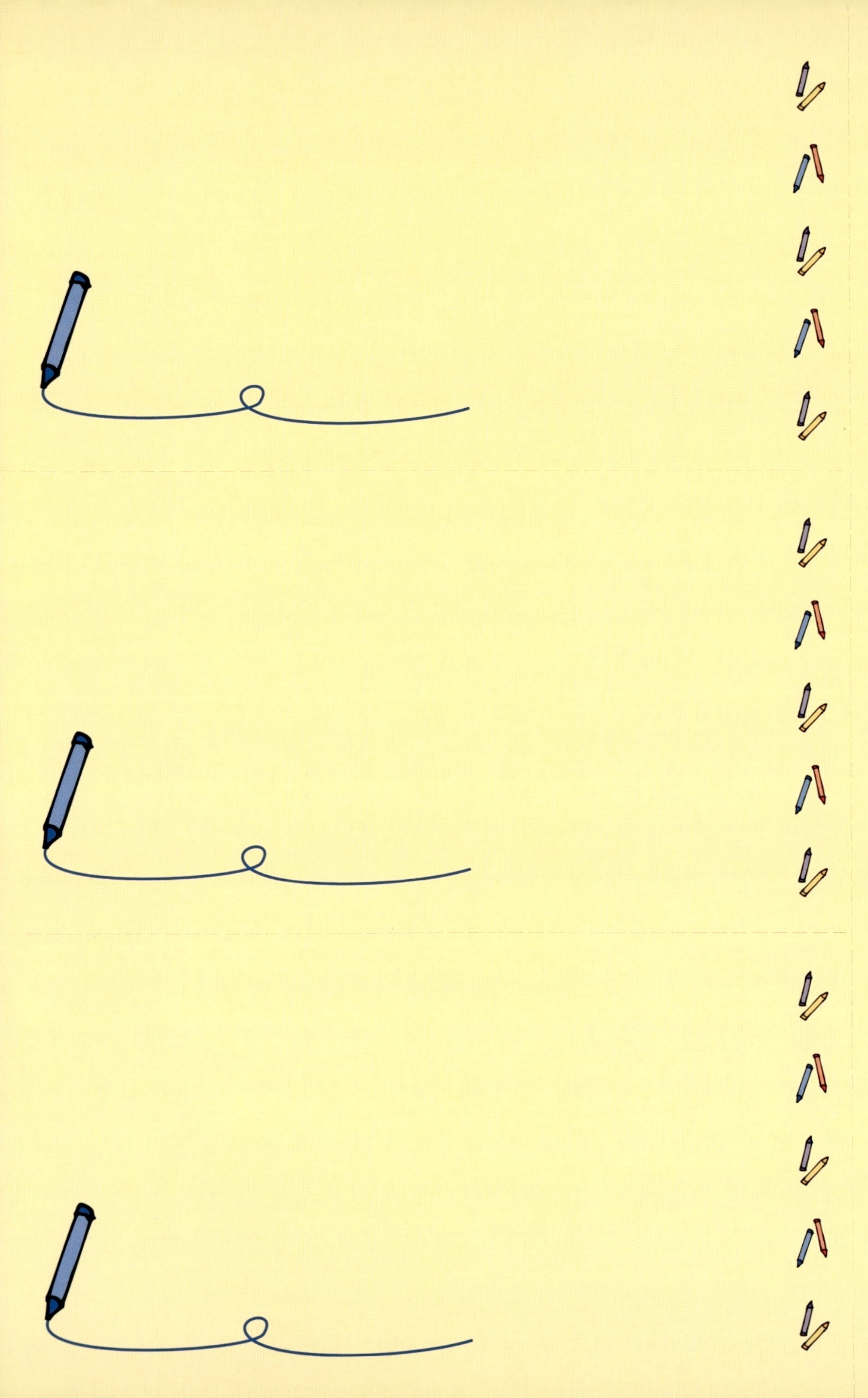

Black & White Cupcake Mix

½ cup granulated sugar
⅓ cup packed brown sugar
1¼ cups all-purpose flour
½ teaspoon baking powder
¼ teaspoon baking soda
¼ teaspoon salt
½ cup unsweetened cocoa powder
1 cup white chocolate chips
¾ cup mini chocolate sandwich cookies (about 36)

Layer ingredients in 1-quart food storage jar with tight-fitting lid in following order: granulated sugar; brown sugar, lightly packed; combined flour, baking powder, baking soda and salt; cocoa; white chocolate chips; and cookies in small plastic bag. Seal jar; cover lid with fabric. Attach gift tag and fabric to jar with raffia.

Makes one 1-quart jar

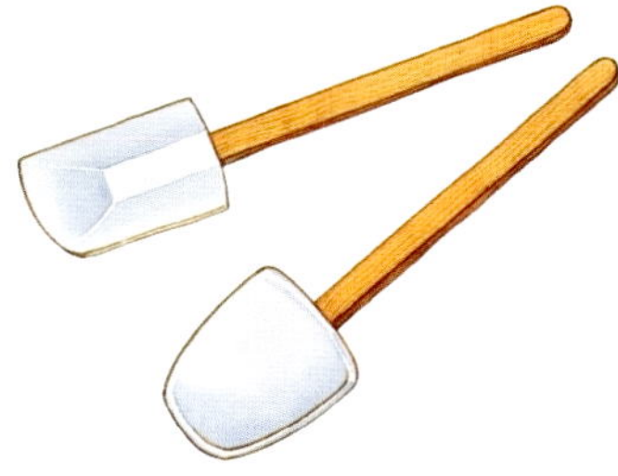

Black & White Cupcakes

½ cup butter (1 stick), softened
2 eggs
1 jar Black & White Cupcake Mix
⅔ cup buttermilk
1 teaspoon vanilla
1 container vanilla frosting

1. Preheat oven to 350°F. Line 18 (2½-inch) muffin cups with paper or foil liners. Remove bag of cookies from jar; set aside.

2. Beat butter 1 minute in medium bowl on medium speed with electric mixer. Add eggs; beat 1 minute. Add contents of jar; beat 30 seconds at low speed. Gradually add buttermilk and vanilla, beating 1½ minutes at medium speed or until well blended.

3. Fill muffin cups ¾ full of batter. Bake 17 to 19 minutes or until cupcakes spring back when lightly touched. Cool completely on wire rack. Frost cupcakes; arrange mini cookies on top of cupcakes.

Makes 18 cupcakes

Black & White Cupcakes

½ cup butter, softened
2 eggs
1 jar Black & White Cupcake Mix
⅔ cup buttermilk
1 teaspoon vanilla
1 container vanilla frosting

1. Preheat oven to 350°F. Line 18 (2½-inch) muffin cups with paper or foil liners. Remove bag of cookies from jar; set aside.
2. Beat butter 1 minute in medium bowl on medium speed with electric mixer. Add eggs; beat 1 minute. Add contents of jar; beat 30 seconds at low speed. Gradually add buttermilk and vanilla, beating 1½ minutes at medium speed or until well blended.
3. Fill muffin cups ¾ full of batter. Bake 17 to 19 minutes or until cupcakes spring back when lightly touched. Cool completely on wire rack. Frost cupcakes; arrange mini cookies on top of cupcakes.

Makes 18 cupcakes

Black & White Cupcakes

½ cup butter, softened
2 eggs
1 jar Black & White Cupcake Mix
⅔ cup buttermilk
1 teaspoon vanilla
1 container vanilla frosting

1. Preheat oven to 350°F. Line 18 (2½-inch) muffin cups with paper or foil liners. Remove bag of cookies from jar; set aside.
2. Beat butter 1 minute in medium bowl on medium speed with electric mixer. Add eggs; beat 1 minute. Add contents of jar; beat 30 seconds at low speed. Gradually add buttermilk and vanilla, beating 1½ minutes at medium speed or until well blended.
3. Fill muffin cups ¾ full of batter. Bake 17 to 19 minutes or until cupcakes spring back when lightly touched. Cool completely on wire rack. Frost cupcakes; arrange mini cookies on top of cupcakes.

Makes 18 cupcakes

Black & White Cupcakes

½ cup butter, softened
2 eggs
1 jar Black & White Cupcake Mix
⅔ cup buttermilk
1 teaspoon vanilla
1 container vanilla frosting

1. Preheat oven to 350°F. Line 18 (2½-inch) muffin cups with paper or foil liners. Remove bag of cookies from jar; set aside.
2. Beat butter 1 minute in medium bowl on medium speed with electric mixer. Add eggs; beat 1 minute. Add contents of jar; beat 30 seconds at low speed. Gradually add buttermilk and vanilla, beating 1½ minutes at medium speed or until well blended.
3. Fill muffin cups ¾ full of batter. Bake 17 to 19 minutes or until cupcakes spring back when lightly touched. Cool completely on wire rack. Frost cupcakes; arrange mini cookies on top of cupcakes.

Makes 18 cupcakes

Black & White Cupcakes

½ cup butter, softened
2 eggs
1 jar Black & White Cupcake Mix
⅔ cup buttermilk
1 teaspoon vanilla
1 container vanilla frosting

1. Preheat oven to 350°F. Line 18 (2½-inch) muffin cups with paper or foil liners. Remove bag of cookies from jar; set aside.
2. Beat butter 1 minute in medium bowl on medium speed with electric mixer. Add eggs; beat 1 minute. Add contents of jar; beat 30 seconds at low speed. Gradually add buttermilk and vanilla, beating 1½ minutes at medium speed or until well blended.
3. Fill muffin cups ¾ full of batter. Bake 17 to 19 minutes or until cupcakes spring back when lightly touched. Cool completely on wire rack. Frost cupcakes; arrange mini cookies on top of cupcakes. *Makes 18 cupcakes*

Black & White Cupcakes

½ cup butter, softened
2 eggs
1 jar Black & White Cupcake Mix
⅔ cup buttermilk
1 teaspoon vanilla
1 container vanilla frosting

1. Preheat oven to 350°F. Line 18 (2½-inch) muffin cups with paper or foil liners. Remove bag of cookies from jar; set aside.
2. Beat butter 1 minute in medium bowl on medium speed with electric mixer. Add eggs; beat 1 minute. Add contents of jar; beat 30 seconds at low speed. Gradually add buttermilk and vanilla, beating 1½ minutes at medium speed or until well blended.
3. Fill muffin cups ¾ full of batter. Bake 17 to 19 minutes or until cupcakes spring back when lightly touched. Cool completely on wire rack. Frost cupcakes; arrange mini cookies on top of cupcakes. *Makes 18 cupcakes*

Black & White Cupcakes

½ cup butter, softened
2 eggs
1 jar Black & White Cupcake Mix
⅔ cup buttermilk
1 teaspoon vanilla
1 container vanilla frosting

1. Preheat oven to 350°F. Line 18 (2½-inch) muffin cups with paper or foil liners. Remove bag of cookies from jar; set aside.
2. Beat butter 1 minute in medium bowl on medium speed with electric mixer. Add eggs; beat 1 minute. Add contents of jar; beat 30 seconds at low speed. Gradually add buttermilk and vanilla, beating 1½ minutes at medium speed or until well blended.
3. Fill muffin cups ¾ full of batter. Bake 17 to 19 minutes or until cupcakes spring back when lightly touched. Cool completely on wire rack. Frost cupcakes; arrange mini cookies on top of cupcakes. *Makes 18 cupcakes*

Oatmeal-Apricot Jammer Mix

- 2/3 cup packed brown sugar
- 1 cup all-purpose flour
- 1/2 teaspoon salt
- 1/2 teaspoon baking powder
- 1/2 teaspoon ground cinnamon
- 1 cup uncooked old-fashioned oats
- 2/3 cup flaked coconut
- 2/3 cup coarsely chopped pecans

Layer ingredients in 1-quart food storage jar with tight-fitting lid in following order: brown sugar, lightly packed; combined flour, salt, baking powder and cinnamon; oats; coconut; and pecans. Seal jar; cover lid with fabric. Attach gift tag and fabric to jar with raffia.

Makes one 1-quart jar

Oatmeal-Apricot Jammers

⅔ cup unsalted butter, softened
1 egg
1 jar Oatmeal-Apricot Jammer Mix
¾ cup apricot jam

1. Preheat oven to 350°F. Grease 9×9-inch baking pan; set aside.

2. Beat butter 1 minute in large bowl with electric mixer at medium speed. Add egg; beat 1 minute. Add contents of jar; beat 2 minutes at low speed until or well blended.

3. Press ⅔ of dough into prepared baking pan. Stir jam until smooth; spread over dough almost to edges of pan. Sprinkle remaining dough over jam; press lightly with fingers.

4. Bake 33 to 35 minutes or until crust is golden brown. Cool completely in pan on wire rack. Cut into bars. *Makes 24 bars*

Oatmeal-Apricot Jammers

$\frac{2}{3}$ cup unsalted butter, softened
1 egg
1 jar Oatmeal-Apricot Jammer Mix
$\frac{3}{4}$ cup apricot jam

1. Preheat oven to 350°F. Grease 9×9-inch baking pan; set aside.

2. Beat butter 1 minute in large bowl with electric mixer at medium speed. Add egg; beat 1 minute. Add contents of jar; beat 2 minutes at low speed or until well blended.

3. Press $\frac{2}{3}$ of dough into prepared baking pan. Stir jam until smooth; spread over dough almost to edges of pan. Sprinkle remaining dough over jam; press lightly with fingers.

4. Bake 33 to 35 minutes or until crust is golden brown. Cool completely in pan on wire rack. Cut into bars.

Makes 24 bars

Oatmeal-Apricot Jammers

$\frac{2}{3}$ cup unsalted butter, softened
1 egg
1 jar Oatmeal-Apricot Jammer Mix
$\frac{3}{4}$ cup apricot jam

1. Preheat oven to 350°F. Grease 9×9-inch baking pan; set aside.
2. Beat butter 1 minute in large bowl with electric mixer at medium speed. Add egg; beat 1 minute. Add contents of jar; beat 2 minutes at low speed or until well blended.
3. Press $\frac{2}{3}$ of dough into prepared baking pan. Stir jam until smooth; spread over dough almost to edges of pan. Sprinkle remaining dough over jam; press lightly with fingers.
4. Bake 33 to 35 minutes or until crust is golden brown. Cool completely in pan on wire rack. Cut into bars.

Makes 24 bars

Oatmeal-Apricot Jammers

$\frac{2}{3}$ cup unsalted butter, softened
1 egg
1 jar Oatmeal-Apricot Jammer Mix
$\frac{3}{4}$ cup apricot jam

1. Preheat oven to 350°F. Grease 9×9-inch baking pan; set aside.
2. Beat butter 1 minute in large bowl with electric mixer at medium speed. Add egg; beat 1 minute. Add contents of jar; beat 2 minutes at low speed or until well blended.
3. Press $\frac{2}{3}$ of dough into prepared baking pan. Stir jam until smooth; spread over dough almost to edges of pan. Sprinkle remaining dough over jam; press lightly with fingers.
4. Bake 33 to 35 minutes or until crust is golden brown. Cool completely in pan on wire rack. Cut into bars.

Makes 24 bars

Oatmeal-Apricot Jammers

⅔ cup unsalted butter, softened
1 egg
1 jar Oatmeal-Apricot Jammer Mix
¾ cup apricot jam

1. Preheat oven to 350°F. Grease 9×9-inch baking pan; set aside.
2. Beat butter 1 minute in large bowl with electric mixer at medium speed. Add egg; beat 1 minute. Add contents of jar; beat 2 minutes at low speed or until well blended.
3. Press ⅔ of dough into prepared baking pan. Stir jam until smooth; spread over dough almost to edges of pan. Sprinkle remaining dough over jam; press lightly with fingers.
4. Bake 33 to 35 minutes or until crust is golden brown. Cool completely in pan on wire rack. Cut into bars.

Makes 24 bars

Oatmeal-Apricot Jammers

⅔ cup unsalted butter, softened
1 egg
1 jar Oatmeal-Apricot Jammer Mix
¾ cup apricot jam

1. Preheat oven to 350°F. Grease 9×9-inch baking pan; set aside.
2. Beat butter 1 minute in large bowl with electric mixer at medium speed. Add egg; beat 1 minute. Add contents of jar; beat 2 minutes at low speed or until well blended.
3. Press ⅔ of dough into prepared baking pan. Stir jam until smooth; spread over dough almost to edges of pan. Sprinkle remaining dough over jam; press lightly with fingers.
4. Bake 33 to 35 minutes or until crust is golden brown. Cool completely in pan on wire rack. Cut into bars.

Makes 24 bars

Oatmeal-Apricot Jammers

⅔ cup unsalted butter, softened
1 egg
1 jar Oatmeal-Apricot Jammer Mix
¾ cup apricot jam

1. Preheat oven to 350°F. Grease 9×9-inch baking pan; set aside.
2. Beat butter 1 minute in large bowl with electric mixer at medium speed. Add egg; beat 1 minute. Add contents of jar; beat 2 minutes at low speed or until well blended.
3. Press ⅔ of dough into prepared baking pan. Stir jam until smooth; spread over dough almost to edges of pan. Sprinkle remaining dough over jam; press lightly with fingers.
4. Bake 33 to 35 minutes or until crust is golden brown. Cool completely in pan on wire rack. Cut into bars.

Makes 24 bars

No-Bake Noodle Cookie Mix

- 2 cups crisp chow mein noodles
- ⅓ cup raisins
- ½ cup cocktail peanuts
- ⅔ cup semisweet chocolate chips
- ½ cup peanut butter chips

Layer ingredients in 1-quart in food storage jar with tight-fitting lid in following order: chow mein noodles; raisins; peanuts; chocolate chips; and peanut butter chips. Seal jar; cover lid with fabric. Attach gift tag and fabric to jar with raffia.

Makes one 1-quart jar

No-Bake Noodle Cookies

1 jar No-Bake Noodle Cookie Mix

1. Line 2 large cookie sheets with waxed paper or parchment paper; set aside.

2. Place contents of jar in large microwavable bowl. Microwave 1 minute at HIGH; stir. If necessary, microwave 30 seconds more or until chips are melted. Stir until well blended.

3. Drop noodle mixture by teaspoonfuls onto prepared cookie sheets. Refrigerate 1 hour. Store cookies between sheets of waxed paper in air-tight storage container; refrigerate.

Makes 2 dozen cookies

No-Bake Noodle Cookies

1 jar No-Bake Noodle Cookie Mix

1. Line 2 large cookie sheets with waxed paper or parchment paper; set aside.
2. Place contents of jar in large microwavable bowl. Microwave 1 minute at HIGH; stir. If necessary, microwave 30 seconds more or until chips are melted. Stir until well blended.
3. Drop noodle mixture by teaspoonfuls onto prepared cookie sheets. Refrigerate 1 hour. Store cookies between sheets of waxed paper in air-tight storage container; refrigerate. *Makes 2 dozen cookies*

No-Bake Noodle Cookies

1 jar No-Bake Noodle Cookie Mix

1. Line 2 large cookie sheets with waxed paper or parchment paper; set aside.
2. Place contents of jar in large microwavable bowl. Microwave 1 minute at HIGH; stir. If necessary, microwave 30 seconds more or until chips are melted. Stir until well blended.
3. Drop noodle mixture by teaspoonfuls onto prepared cookie sheets. Refrigerate 1 hour. Store cookies between sheets of waxed paper in air-tight storage container; refrigerate. *Makes 2 dozen cookies*

No-Bake Noodle Cookies

1 jar No-Bake Noodle Cookie Mix

1. Line 2 large cookie sheets with waxed paper or parchment paper; set aside.
2. Place contents of jar in large microwavable bowl. Microwave 1 minute at HIGH; stir. If necessary, microwave 30 seconds more or until chips are melted. Stir until well blended.
3. Drop noodle mixture by teaspoonfuls onto prepared cookie sheets. Refrigerate 1 hour. Store cookies between sheets of waxed paper in air-tight storage container; refrigerate. *Makes 2 dozen cookies*

No-Bake Noodle Cookies

1 jar No-Bake Noodle Cookie Mix

1. Line 2 large cookie sheets with waxed paper or parchment paper; set aside.
2. Place contents of jar in large microwavable bowl. Microwave 1 minute at HIGH; stir. If necessary, microwave 30 seconds more or until chips are melted. Stir until well blended.
3. Drop noodle mixture by teaspoonfuls onto prepared cookie sheets. Refrigerate 1 hour. Store cookies between sheets of waxed paper in air-tight storage container; refrigerate. *Makes 2 dozen cookies*

No-Bake Noodle Cookies

1 jar No-Bake Noodle Cookie Mix

1. Line 2 large cookie sheets with waxed paper or parchment paper; set aside.
2. Place contents of jar in large microwavable bowl. Microwave 1 minute at HIGH; stir. If necessary, microwave 30 seconds more or until chips are melted. Stir until well blended.
3. Drop noodle mixture by teaspoonfuls onto prepared cookie sheets. Refrigerate 1 hour. Store cookies between sheets of waxed paper in air-tight storage container; refrigerate. *Makes 2 dozen cookies*

No-Bake Noodle Cookies

1 jar No-Bake Noodle Cookie Mix

1. Line 2 large cookie sheets with waxed paper or parchment paper; set aside.
2. Place contents of jar in large microwavable bowl. Microwave 1 minute at HIGH; stir. If necessary, microwave 30 seconds more or until chips are melted. Stir until well blended.
3. Drop noodle mixture by teaspoonfuls onto prepared cookie sheets. Refrigerate 1 hour. Store cookies between sheets of waxed paper in air-tight storage container; refrigerate. *Makes 2 dozen cookies*

Chocolate-Toffee Bar Mix

¼ cup granulated sugar
½ cup packed brown sugar
2¼ cups all-purpose flour
¼ teaspoon salt
2½ cups semisweet chocolate chips, divided
½ cup toffee baking bits

Layer ingredients in 1½-quart food storage jar with tight-fitting lid in following order: granulated sugar; brown sugar, lightly packed; flour and salt; 1½ cups chocolate chips; toffee bits and remaining 1 cup chocolate chips in small plastic bag. Seal jar; cover lid with fabric. Attach gift tag and fabric to jar with raffia.

Makes one 1½-quart jar

Chocolate-Toffee Bars

¾ cup (1½ sticks) butter, softened
1 jar Chocolate-Toffee Bar Mix
1 egg
1 can (14 ounces) sweetened condensed milk

1. Preheat oven to 350°F. Grease 13×9-inch baking pan; set aside.

2. Remove bag from jar; set aside. Beat butter 1 minute in large bowl with electric mixer at medium speed. Add remaining contents of jar and egg. Beat 30 seconds at low speed. Beat 1½ minutes at medium speed or until well blended.

3. Reserve about 1½ cups dough. Press remaining dough into bottom of prepared pan. Bake 15 minutes. Remove from oven.

4. Pour condensed milk evenly over hot crust. Drop bits of reserved dough over milk. Sprinkle contents of bag over dough; press lightly. Bake 20 to 25 minutes or until lightly browned on top. *Do not overbake*. Cool completely in pan on wire rack. Cut into bars.

Makes about 4 dozen bars

Chocolate-Toffee Bars

- ¾ cup (1½ sticks) butter, softened
- 1 jar Chocolate-Toffee Bar Mix
- 1 egg
- 1 can (14 ounces) sweetened condensed milk

1. Preheat oven to 350°F. Grease 13×9-inch baking pan; set aside.
2. Remove bag from jar; set aside. Beat butter 1 minute in large bowl with electric mixer at medium speed. Add remaining contents of jar and egg. Beat 30 seconds at low speed. Beat 1½ minutes at medium speed or until well blended.
3. Reserve about 1½ cups dough. Press remaining dough into bottom of prepared pan. Bake 15 minutes. Remove from oven.

4. Pour condensed milk evenly over hot crust. Drop bits of reserved dough over milk. Sprinkle contents of bag over dough; press lightly. Bake 20 to 25 minutes or until lightly browned on top. *Do not overbake*. Cool completely in pan on wire rack. Cut into bars.

Makes about 4 dozen bars

Chocolate-Toffee Bars

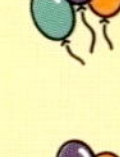

- ¾ cup (1½ sticks) butter, softened
- 1 jar Chocolate-Toffee Bar Mix
- 1 egg
- 1 can (14 ounces) sweetened condensed milk

1. Preheat oven to 350°F. Grease 13×9-inch baking pan; set aside.
2. Remove bag from jar; set aside. Beat butter 1 minute in large bowl with electric mixer at medium speed. Add remaining contents of jar and egg. Beat 30 seconds at low speed. Beat 1½ minutes at medium speed or until well blended.
3. Reserve about 1½ cups dough. Press remaining dough into bottom of prepared pan. Bake 15 minutes. Remove from oven.
4. Pour condensed milk evenly over hot crust. Drop bits of reserved dough over milk. Sprinkle contents of bag over dough; press lightly. Bake 20 to 25 minutes or until lightly browned on top. *Do not overbake*. Cool completely in pan on wire rack. Cut into bars.

Makes about 4 dozen bars

Chocolate-Toffee Bars

- ¾ cup (1½ sticks) butter, softened
- 1 jar Chocolate-Toffee Bar Mix
- 1 egg
- 1 can (14 ounces) sweetened condensed milk

1. Preheat oven to 350°F. Grease 13×9-inch baking pan; set aside.
2. Remove bag from jar; set aside. Beat butter 1 minute in large bowl with electric mixer at medium speed. Add remaining contents of jar and egg. Beat 30 seconds at low speed. Beat 1½ minutes at medium speed or until well blended.
3. Reserve about 1½ cups dough. Press remaining dough into bottom of prepared pan. Bake 15 minutes. Remove from oven.
4. Pour condensed milk evenly over hot crust. Drop bits of reserved dough over milk. Sprinkle contents of bag over dough; press lightly. Bake 20 to 25 minutes or until lightly browned on top. *Do not overbake*. Cool completely in pan on wire rack. Cut into bars.

Makes about 4 dozen bars

Chocolate-Toffee Bars

¾ cup (1½ sticks) butter, softened
1 jar Chocolate-Toffee Bar Mix
1 egg
1 can (14 ounces) sweetened condensed milk

1. Preheat oven to 350°F. Grease 13×9-inch baking pan; set aside.
2. Remove bag from jar; set aside. Beat butter 1 minute in large bowl with electric mixer at medium speed. Add remaining contents of jar and egg. Beat 30 seconds at low speed. Beat 1½ minutes at medium speed or until well blended.
3. Reserve about 1½ cups dough. Press remaining dough into bottom of prepared pan. Bake 15 minutes. Remove from oven.
4. Pour condensed milk evenly over hot crust. Drop bits of reserved dough over milk. Sprinkle contents of bag over dough; press lightly. Bake 20 to 25 minutes or until lightly browned on top. *Do not overbake*. Cool completely in pan on wire rack. Cut into bars.

Makes about 4 dozen bars

Chocolate-Toffee Bars

¾ cup (1½ sticks) butter, softened
1 jar Chocolate-Toffee Bar Mix
1 egg
1 can (14 ounces) sweetened condensed milk

1. Preheat oven to 350°F. Grease 13×9-inch baking pan; set aside.
2. Remove bag from jar; set aside. Beat butter 1 minute in large bowl with electric mixer at medium speed. Add remaining contents of jar and egg. Beat 30 seconds at low speed. Beat 1½ minutes at medium speed or until well blended.
3. Reserve about 1½ cups dough. Press remaining dough into bottom of prepared pan. Bake 15 minutes. Remove from oven.
4. Pour condensed milk evenly over hot crust. Drop bits of reserved dough over milk. Sprinkle contents of bag over dough; press lightly. Bake 20 to 25 minutes or until lightly browned on top. *Do not overbake*. Cool completely in pan on wire rack. Cut into bars.

Makes about 4 dozen bars

Chocolate-Toffee Bars

¾ cup (1½ sticks) butter, softened
1 jar Chocolate-Toffee Bar Mix
1 egg
1 can (14 ounces) sweetened condensed milk

1. Preheat oven to 350°F. Grease 13×9-inch baking pan; set aside.
2. Remove bag from jar; set aside. Beat butter 1 minute in large bowl with electric mixer at medium speed. Add remaining contents of jar and egg. Beat 30 seconds at low speed. Beat 1½ minutes at medium speed or until well blended.
3. Reserve about 1½ cups dough. Press remaining dough into bottom of prepared pan. Bake 15 minutes. Remove from oven.
4. Pour condensed milk evenly over hot crust. Drop bits of reserved dough over milk. Sprinkle contents of bag over dough; press lightly. Bake 20 to 25 minutes or until lightly browned on top. *Do not overbake*. Cool completely in pan on wire rack. Cut into bars.

Makes about 4 dozen bars

Oatmeal-Chip Crispies Mix

¾ cup granulated sugar
1 cup packed brown sugar
2 cups all-purpose flour
1 teaspoon baking powder
1 teaspoon baking soda
½ teaspoon salt
2 cups uncooked old-fashioned oats
1 cup dried cranberries
⅔ cup white chocolate chips*
⅔ cup semisweet chocolate chips

*Semisweet chocolate chips can be substituted for the white chocolate chips. Instead, use 1⅓ cups semisweet chocolate chips.

Layer ingredients in ½-gallon food storage jar with tight-fitting lid in following order: granulated sugar; brown sugar, lightly packed; combined flour, baking powder, baking soda and salt; oats; cranberries; white chocolate chips; and semisweet chocolate chips. Seal jar; cover lid with fabric. Attach gift tag and fabric to jar with raffia.

Makes one ½ gallon jar

Oatmeal-Chip Crispies

1 cup (2 sticks) unsalted butter, softened
2 eggs
2 tablespoons orange juice
1 teaspoon grated orange peel
1 jar Oatmeal-Chip Crispies Mix

1. Preheat oven to 350°F. Grease cookie sheets.

2. Beat butter 1 minute in large bowl with electric mixer at medium speed. Add eggs, orange juice and peel; beat 1 minute. Add contents of jar; beat 30 seconds on low speed. Beat 1 minute at medium speed or until well blended.

3. Shape dough into 1-inch balls. Place 1½ inches apart onto prepared cookie sheets. Flatten slightly to ⅜-inch thickness. Bake 15 to 17 minutes or until lightly browned and firm to the touch. Cool cookies on cookie sheets 2 minutes. Remove to wire rack; cool completely. *Makes about 6 dozen cookies*

Oatmeal-Chip Crispies

1 cup (2 sticks) unsalted butter, softened
2 eggs
2 tablespoons orange juice
1 teaspoon grated orange peel
1 jar Oatmeal-Chip Crispies Mix

1. Preheat oven to 350°F. Grease cookie sheets.
2. Beat butter 1 minute in large bowl with electric mixer at medium speed. Add eggs, orange juice and peel; beat 1 minute. Add contents of jar; beat 30 seconds on low speed. Beat 1 minute at medium speed or until well blended.
3. Shape dough into 1-inch balls. Place 1½ inches apart onto prepared cookie sheets. Flatten slightly to ⅜-inch thickness. Bake 15 to 17 minutes or until lightly browned and firm to the touch. Cool cookies on cookie sheets 2 minutes. Remove to wire rack; cool completely.

Makes about 6 dozen cookies

Oatmeal-Chip Crispies

1 cup (2 sticks) unsalted butter, softened
2 eggs
2 tablespoons orange juice
1 teaspoon grated orange peel
1 jar Oatmeal-Chip Crispies Mix

1. Preheat oven to 350°F. Grease cookie sheets.
2. Beat butter 1 minute in large bowl with electric mixer at medium speed. Add eggs, orange juice and peel; beat 1 minute. Add contents of jar; beat 30 seconds on low speed. Beat 1 minute at medium speed or until well blended.
3. Shape dough into 1-inch balls. Place 1½ inches apart onto prepared cookie sheets. Flatten slightly to ⅜-inch thickness. Bake 15 to 17 minutes or until lightly browned and firm to the touch. Cool cookies on cookie sheets 2 minutes. Remove to wire rack; cool completely.

Makes about 6 dozen cookies

Oatmeal-Chip Crispies

1 cup (2 sticks) unsalted butter, softened
2 eggs
2 tablespoons orange juice
1 teaspoon grated orange peel
1 jar Oatmeal-Chip Crispies Mix

1. Preheat oven to 350°F. Grease cookie sheets.
2. Beat butter 1 minute in large bowl with electric mixer at medium speed. Add eggs, orange juice and peel; beat 1 minute. Add contents of jar; beat 30 seconds on low speed. Beat 1 minute at medium speed or until well blended.
3. Shape dough into 1-inch balls. Place 1½ inches apart onto prepared cookie sheets. Flatten slightly to ⅜-inch thickness. Bake 15 to 17 minutes or until lightly browned and firm to the touch. Cool cookies on cookie sheets 2 minutes. Remove to wire rack; cool completely.

Makes about 6 dozen cookies

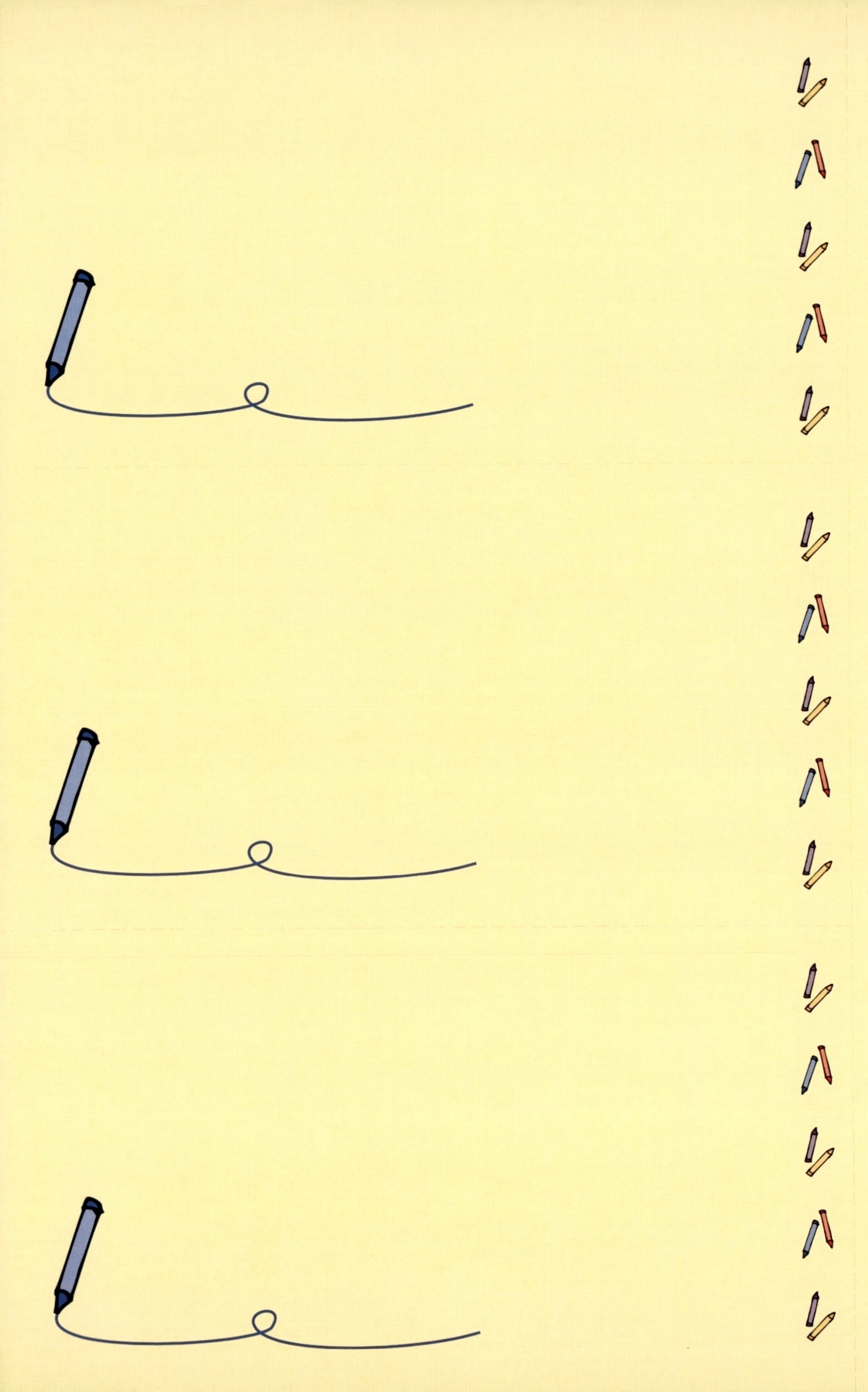

Oatmeal-Chip Crispies

1 cup (2 sticks) unsalted butter, softened
2 eggs
2 tablespoons orange juice
1 teaspoon grated orange peel
1 jar Oatmeal-Chip Crispies Mix

1. Preheat oven to 350°F. Grease cookie sheets.
2. Beat butter 1 minute in large bowl with electric mixer at medium speed. Add eggs, orange juice and peel; beat 1 minute. Add contents of jar; beat 30 seconds on low speed. Beat 1 minute at medium speed or until well blended.
3. Shape dough into 1-inch balls. Place 1½ inches apart onto prepared cookie sheets. Flatten slightly to ⅜-inch thickness. Bake 15 to 17 minutes or until lightly browned and firm to the touch. Cool cookies on cookie sheets 2 minutes. Remove to wire rack; cool completely. *Makes about 6 dozen cookies*

Oatmeal-Chip Crispies

1 cup (2 sticks) unsalted butter, softened
2 eggs
2 tablespoons orange juice
1 teaspoon grated orange peel
1 jar Oatmeal-Chip Crispies Mix

1. Preheat oven to 350°F. Grease cookie sheets.
2. Beat butter 1 minute in large bowl with electric mixer at medium speed. Add eggs, orange juice and peel; beat 1 minute. Add contents of jar; beat 30 seconds on low speed. Beat 1 minute at medium speed or until well blended.
3. Shape dough into 1-inch balls. Place 1½ inches apart onto prepared cookie sheets. Flatten slightly to ⅜-inch thickness. Bake 15 to 17 minutes or until lightly browned and firm to the touch. Cool cookies on cookie sheets 2 minutes. Remove to wire rack; cool completely. *Makes about 6 dozen cookies*

Oatmeal-Chip Crispies

1 cup (2 sticks) unsalted butter, softened
2 eggs
2 tablespoons orange juice
1 teaspoon grated orange peel
1 jar Oatmeal-Chip Crispies Mix

1. Preheat oven to 350°F. Grease cookie sheets.
2. Beat butter 1 minute in large bowl with electric mixer at medium speed. Add eggs, orange juice and peel; beat 1 minute. Add contents of jar; beat 30 seconds on low speed. Beat 1 minute at medium speed or until well blended.
3. Shape dough into 1-inch balls. Place 1½ inches apart onto prepared cookie sheets. Flatten slightly to ⅜-inch thickness. Bake 15 to 17 minutes or until lightly browned and firm to the touch. Cool cookies on cookie sheets 2 minutes. Remove to wire rack; cool completely. *Makes about 6 dozen cookies*

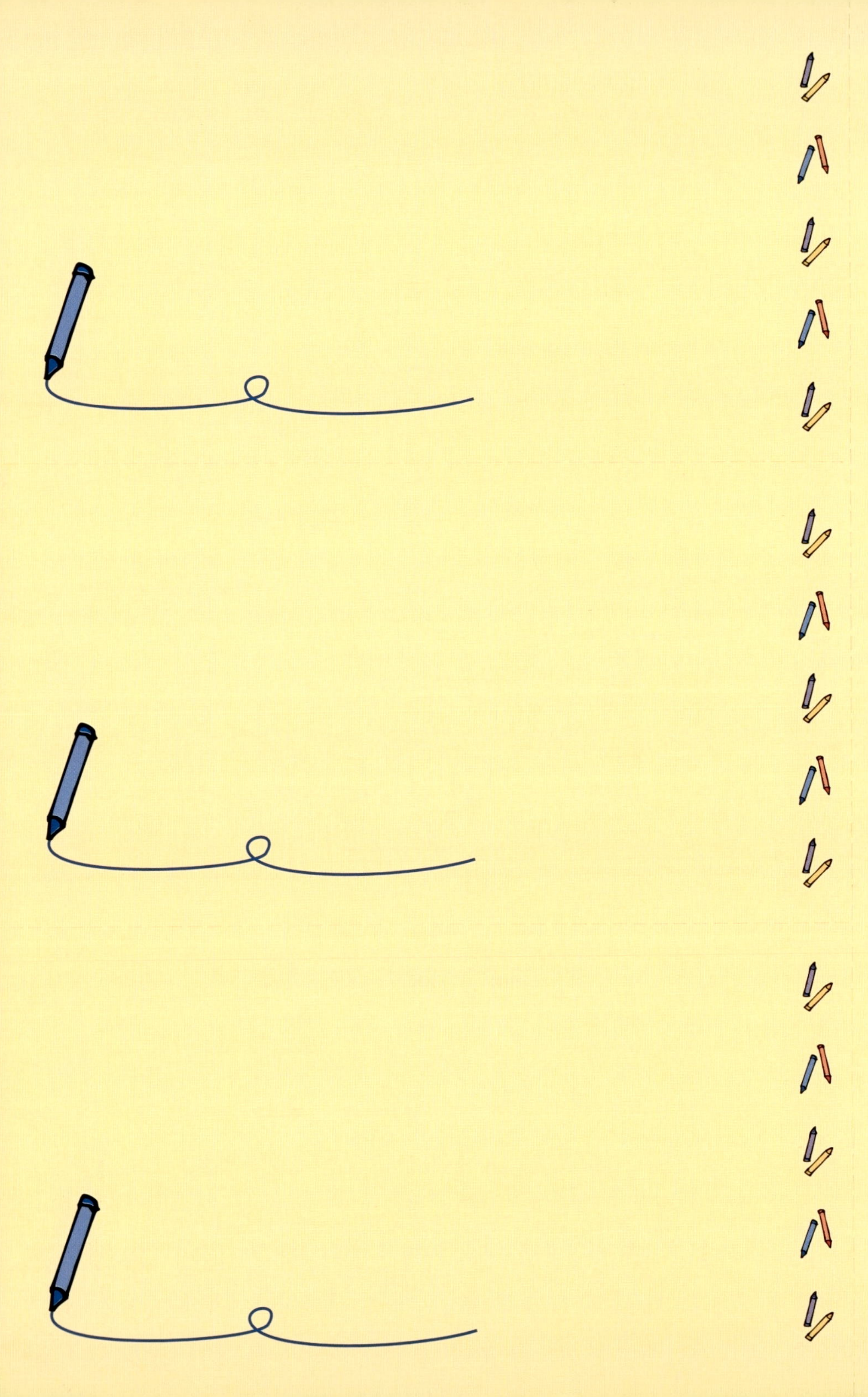

Italian Parmesan Snack Mix

1 cup oyster crackers
1¼ cups Parmesan-flavored mini fish-shaped crackers
1½ cups small bow-tie pretzels
2 tablespoons grated Parmesan cheese
1½ teaspoons Italian seasoning
¼ teaspoon garlic powder

Layer ingredients in 1-quart food storage jar with tight-fitting lid in following order: oyster crackers; fish-shaped crackers; pretzels; and combined cheese, Italian seasoning and garlic powder in small plastic bag. Seal jar; cover lid with fabric. Attach gift tag and fabric to jar with raffia.

Makes one 1-quart jar

Italian Parmesan Snack Mix

1 jar Italian Parmesan Snack Mix
2 teaspoons butter or margarine
1 teaspoon olive oil

1. Preheat oven to 250°F. Spray 13×9-inch baking pan with nonstick cooking spray.

2. Remove bag from jar; set aside. Place remaining contents of jar in large bowl.

3. Place butter, oil and contents of plastic bag in small microwavable bowl. Microwave at MEDIUM (50%) 1 minute or until foamy; stir. Pour over contents of jar; stir until blended.

4. Transfer to prepared pan. Bake 10 minutes; stir. Bake 5 minutes more. Cool completely. Store in airtight container.

Makes 4 cups mix

Italian Parmesan Snack Mix

1 jar Italian Parmesan Snack Mix
2 teaspoons butter or margarine
1 teaspoon olive oil

1. Preheat oven to 250°F. Spray 13×9-inch baking pan with nonstick cooking spray.
2. Remove bag from jar; set aside. Place remaining contents of jar in large bowl.
3. Place butter, oil and contents of plastic bag in small microwavable bowl. Microwave at MEDIUM (50%) 1 minute or until foamy; stir. Pour over contents of jar; stir until blended.
4. Transfer to prepared pan. Bake 10 minutes; stir. Bake 5 minutes more. Cool completely. Store in airtight container.

Makes 4 cups mix

Italian Parmesan Snack Mix

1 jar Italian Parmesan Snack Mix
2 teaspoons butter or margarine
1 teaspoon olive oil

1. Preheat oven to 250°F. Spray 13×9-inch baking pan with nonstick cooking spray.
2. Remove bag from jar; set aside. Place remaining contents of jar in large bowl.
3. Place butter, oil and contents of plastic bag in small microwavable bowl. Microwave at MEDIUM (50%) 1 minute or until foamy; stir. Pour over contents of jar; stir until blended.
4. Transfer to prepared pan. Bake 10 minutes; stir. Bake 5 minutes more. Cool completely. Store in airtight container.

Makes 4 cups mix

Italian Parmesan Snack Mix

1 jar Italian Parmesan Snack Mix
2 teaspoons butter or margarine
1 teaspoon olive oil

1. Preheat oven to 250°F. Spray 13×9-inch baking pan with nonstick cooking spray.
2. Remove bag from jar; set aside. Place remaining contents of jar in large bowl.
3. Place butter, oil and contents of plastic bag in small microwavable bowl. Microwave at MEDIUM (50%) 1 minute or until foamy; stir. Pour over contents of jar; stir until blended.
4. Transfer to prepared pan. Bake 10 minutes; stir. Bake 5 minutes more. Cool completely. Store in airtight container.

Makes 4 cups mix

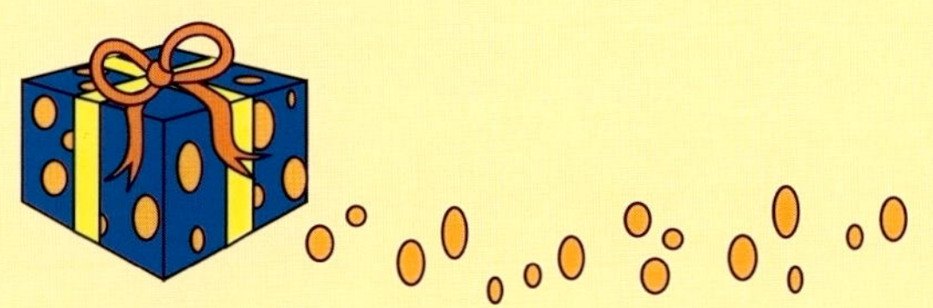

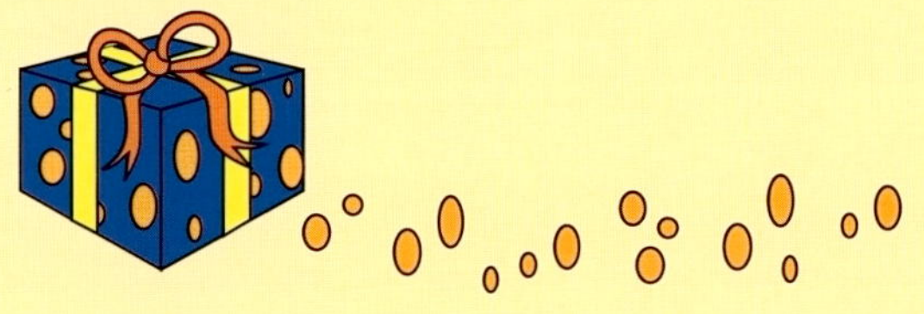

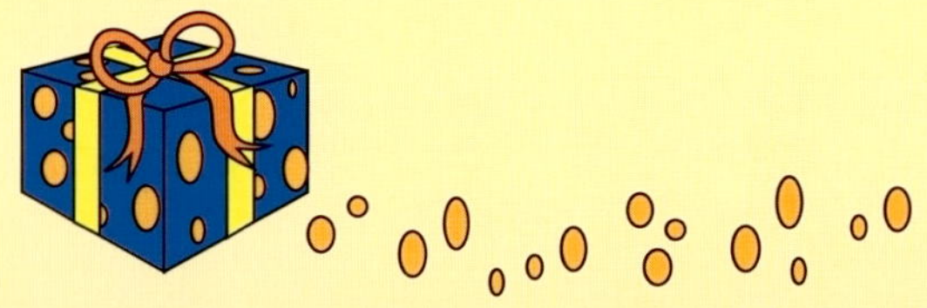

Italian Parmesan Snack Mix

- 1 jar Italian Parmesan Snack Mix
- 2 teaspoons butter or margarine
- 1 teaspoon olive oil

1. Preheat oven to 250°F. Spray 13×9-inch baking pan with nonstick cooking spray.
2. Remove bag from jar; set aside. Place remaining contents of jar in large bowl.
3. Place butter, oil and contents of plastic bag in small microwavable bowl. Microwave at MEDIUM (50%) 1 minute or until foamy; stir. Pour over contents of jar; stir until blended.
4. Transfer to prepared pan. Bake 10 minutes; stir. Bake 5 minutes more. Cool completely. Store in airtight container.

Makes 4 cups mix

Italian Parmesan Snack Mix

- 1 jar Italian Parmesan Snack Mix
- 2 teaspoons butter or margarine
- 1 teaspoon olive oil

1. Preheat oven to 250°F. Spray 13×9-inch baking pan with nonstick cooking spray.
2. Remove bag from jar; set aside. Place remaining contents of jar in large bowl.
3. Place butter, oil and contents of plastic bag in small microwavable bowl. Microwave at MEDIUM (50%) 1 minute or until foamy; stir. Pour over contents of jar; stir until blended.
4. Transfer to prepared pan. Bake 10 minutes; stir. Bake 5 minutes more. Cool completely. Store in airtight container.

Makes 4 cups mix

Italian Parmesan Snack Mix

- 1 jar Italian Parmesan Snack Mix
- 2 teaspoons butter or margarine
- 1 teaspoon olive oil

1. Preheat oven to 250°F. Spray 13×9-inch baking pan with nonstick cooking spray.
2. Remove bag from jar; set aside. Place remaining contents of jar in large bowl.
3. Place butter, oil and contents of plastic bag in small microwavable bowl. Microwave at MEDIUM (50%) 1 minute or until foamy; stir. Pour over contents of jar; stir until blended.
4. Transfer to prepared pan. Bake 10 minutes; stir. Bake 5 minutes more. Cool completely. Store in airtight container.

Makes 4 cups mix

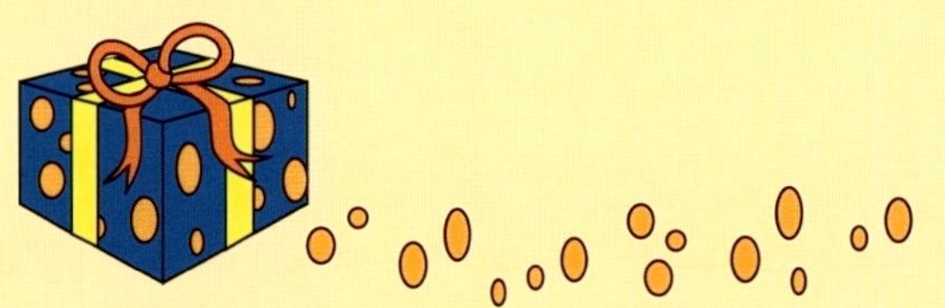

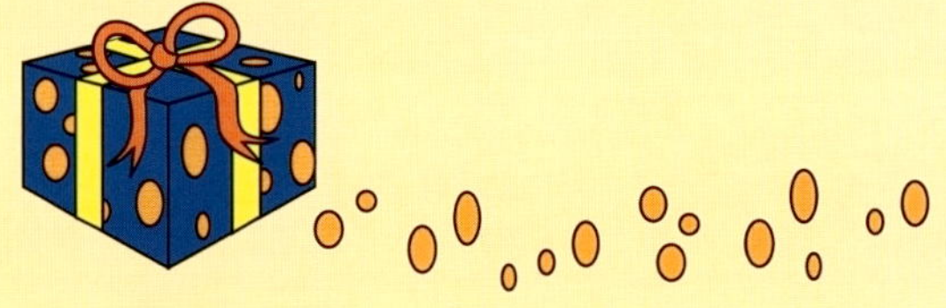

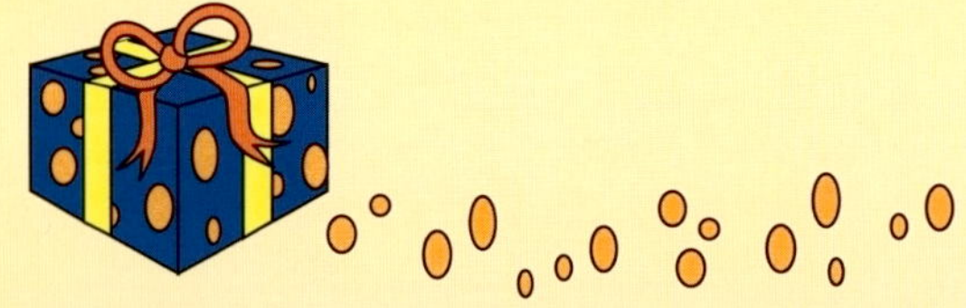

Double Nutter Cookie Mix

- 1½ cups all-purpose flour
- ½ teaspoon salt
- ½ teaspoon baking powder
- ½ teaspoon baking soda
- 1 cup packed brown sugar
- ¾ cup semisweet chocolate chips
- ¾ cup peanut butter chips

Layer ingredients in 1-quart food storage jar with tight-fitting lid in following order: combined flour, salt, baking powder and baking soda; brown sugar, lightly packed; chocolate chips; and peanut butter chips. Seal jar; cover lid with fabric. Attach gift tag and fabric to jar with raffia.

Makes one 1-quart jar

Double Nutter Cookies

½ cup plus 3 tablespoons unsalted butter, softened
½ cup creamy peanut butter
1 egg
1 jar Double Nutter Cookie Mix

1. Preheat oven to 375°F. Grease cookie sheets.

2. Beat butter and peanut butter 1 minute in large bowl with electric mixer at medium speed. Beat in egg until well blended. Add contents of jar; beat on low speed 30 seconds or until blended. Beat 1 to 2 minutes on medium speed or until well blended.

3. Form dough into 1-inch balls. Place 1½ inches apart on prepared cookie sheets. Flatten dough with fork in criss-cross fashion to ½-inch thickness. Bake 11 to 14 minutes or until lightly browned. Cool 2 minutes on cookie sheets. Remove to wire rack; cool completely.

Makes about 5 dozen cookies

Double Nutter Cookies

½ cup plus 3 tablespoons unsalted butter, softened
½ cup creamy peanut butter
1 egg
1 jar Double Nutter Cookie Mix

1. Preheat oven to 375°F. Grease cookie sheets.
2. Beat butter and peanut butter 1 minute in large bowl with electric mixer at medium speed. Beat in egg until well blended. Add contents of jar; beat on low speed 30 seconds or until blended. Beat 1 to 2 minutes on medium speed or until well blended.
3. Form dough into 1-inch balls. Place 1½ inches apart on prepared cookie sheets. Flatten dough with fork in criss-cross fashion to ½-inch thickness. Bake 11 to 14 minutes or until lightly browned. Cool 2 minutes on cookie sheets. Remove to wire rack; cool completely. *Makes about 5 dozen cookies*

Double Nutter Cookies

½ cup plus 3 tablespoons unsalted butter, softened
½ cup creamy peanut butter
1 egg
1 jar Double Nutter Cookie Mix

1. Preheat oven to 375°F. Grease cookie sheets.
2. Beat butter and peanut butter 1 minute in large bowl with electric mixer at medium speed. Beat in egg until well blended. Add contents of jar; beat on low speed 30 seconds or until blended. Beat 1 to 2 minutes on medium speed or until well blended.
3. Form dough into 1-inch balls. Place 1½ inches apart on prepared cookie sheets. Flatten dough with fork in criss-cross fashion to ½-inch thickness. Bake 11 to 14 minutes or until lightly browned. Cool 2 minutes on cookie sheets. Remove to wire rack; cool completely. *Makes about 5 dozen cookies*

Double Nutter Cookies

½ cup plus 3 tablespoons unsalted butter, softened
½ cup creamy peanut butter
1 egg
1 jar Double Nutter Cookie Mix

1. Preheat oven to 375°F. Grease cookie sheets.
2. Beat butter and peanut butter 1 minute in large bowl with electric mixer at medium speed. Beat in egg until well blended. Add contents of jar; beat on low speed 30 seconds or until blended. Beat 1 to 2 minutes on medium speed or until well blended.
3. Form dough into 1-inch balls. Place 1½ inches apart on prepared cookie sheets. Flatten dough with fork in criss-cross fashion to ½-inch thickness. Bake 11 to 14 minutes or until lightly browned. Cool 2 minutes on cookie sheets. Remove to wire rack; cool completely. *Makes about 5 dozen cookies*

Double Nutter Cookies

½ cup plus 3 tablespoons unsalted butter, softened
½ cup creamy peanut butter
1 egg
1 jar Double Nutter Cookie Mix

1. Preheat oven to 375°F. Grease cookie sheets.
2. Beat butter and peanut butter 1 minute in large bowl with electric mixer at medium speed. Beat in egg until well blended. Add contents of jar; beat on low speed 30 seconds or until blended. Beat 1 to 2 minutes on medium speed or until well blended.
3. Form dough into 1-inch balls. Place 1½ inches apart on prepared cookie sheets. Flatten dough with fork in criss-cross fashion to ½-inch thickness. Bake 11 to 14 minutes or until lightly browned. Cool 2 minutes on cookie sheets. Remove to wire rack; cool completely. *Makes about 5 dozen cookies*

Double Nutter Cookies

½ cup plus 3 tablespoons unsalted butter, softened
½ cup creamy peanut butter
1 egg
1 jar Double Nutter Cookie Mix

1. Preheat oven to 375°F. Grease cookie sheets.
2. Beat butter and peanut butter 1 minute in large bowl with electric mixer at medium speed. Beat in egg until well blended. Add contents of jar; beat on low speed 30 seconds or until blended. Beat 1 to 2 minutes on medium speed or until well blended.
3. Form dough into 1-inch balls. Place 1½ inches apart on prepared cookie sheets. Flatten dough with fork in criss-cross fashion to ½-inch thickness. Bake 11 to 14 minutes or until lightly browned. Cool 2 minutes on cookie sheets. Remove to wire rack; cool completely. *Makes about 5 dozen cookies*

Double Nutter Cookies

½ cup plus 3 tablespoons unsalted butter, softened
½ cup creamy peanut butter
1 egg
1 jar Double Nutter Cookie Mix

1. Preheat oven to 375°F. Grease cookie sheets.
2. Beat butter and peanut butter 1 minute in large bowl with electric mixer at medium speed. Beat in egg until well blended. Add contents of jar; beat on low speed 30 seconds or until blended. Beat 1 to 2 minutes on medium speed or until well blended.
3. Form dough into 1-inch balls. Place 1½ inches apart on prepared cookie sheets. Flatten dough with fork in criss-cross fashion to ½-inch thickness. Bake 11 to 14 minutes or until lightly browned. Cool 2 minutes on cookie sheets. Remove to wire rack; cool completely. *Makes about 5 dozen cookies*

Chocolate-Cherry Cupcake Mix

- ⅔ cup granulated sugar
- ⅓ cup packed brown sugar
- 1⅓ cups all-purpose flour
- ½ teaspoon baking powder
- ¼ teaspoon baking soda
- ¼ teaspoon salt
- ½ cup unsweetened cocoa powder
- ⅔ cup dried cherries or cranberries
- ¾ cup semisweet chocolate chips

Layer ingredients in 1-quart food storage jar with tight-fitting lid in following order: granulated sugar; brown sugar, lightly packed; combined flour, baking powder, baking soda and salt; cocoa; cherries; and chocolate chips. Seal jar; cover lid with fabric. Attach gift tag and fabric to jar with raffia. *Makes one 1-quart jar*

Gift Idea: Assemble a gift basket with a jar of Chocolate-Cherry Cupcake Mix, a container of frosting, and paper or foil muffin-cup liners. Complete the basket with a jar of maraschino cherries with stems (to decorate the tops of the cupcakes), a small metal spatula and small colorful paper napkins.

Chocolate-Cherry Cupcakes

2 eggs
⅔ cup buttermilk
¼ cup vegetable oil
1 teaspoon vanilla
1 jar Chocolate-Cherry Cupcake Mix
Frosting (optional)

1. Preheat oven to 350°F. Line 14 (2¾-inch) or 18 (2½-inch) muffin cups with paper or foil liners.

2. Beat eggs in small bowl; stir in buttermilk, oil and vanilla.

3. Place contents of jar in large bowl. Add egg mixture; beat on medium speed of electric mixer 1½ to 2 minutes or until blended. Spoon batter into muffin cups, filling ¾ full. Bake 20 to 21 minutes (for 2¾-inch cups) or 17 to 19 minutes (for 2½-inch cups) or until cupcakes spring back when lightly touched. Cool completely in pans on wire rack. Frost, if desired.

Makes 14 (2¾-inch) cupcakes

Chocolate-Cherry Cupcakes

2 eggs
⅔ cup buttermilk
¼ cup vegetable oil
1 teaspoon vanilla
1 jar Chocolate-Cherry Cupcake Mix
Frosting (optional)

1. Preheat oven to 350°F. Line 14 (2¾-inch) or 18 (2½-inch) muffin cups with paper or foil liners.
2. Beat eggs in small bowl; stir in buttermilk, oil and vanilla.
3. Place contents of jar in large bowl. Add egg mixture; beat on medium speed of electric mixer 1½ to 2 minutes or until blended. Spoon batter into muffin cups, filling ¾ full. Bake 20 to 21 minutes (for 2¾-inch cups) or 17 to 19 minutes (for 2½-inch cups) or until cupcakes spring back when lightly touched. Cool completely in pans on wire rack. Frost, if desired.

Makes 14 (2¾-inch) cupcakes

Chocolate-Cherry Cupcakes

2 eggs
⅔ cup buttermilk
¼ cup vegetable oil
1 teaspoon vanilla
1 jar Chocolate-Cherry Cupcake Mix
Frosting (optional)

1. Preheat oven to 350°F. Line 14 (2¾-inch) or 18 (2½-inch) muffin cups with paper or foil liners.
2. Beat eggs in small bowl; stir in buttermilk, oil and vanilla.
3. Place contents of jar in large bowl. Add egg mixture; beat on medium speed of electric mixer 1½ to 2 minutes or until blended. Spoon batter into muffin cups, filling ¾ full. Bake 20 to 21 minutes (for 2¾-inch cups) or 17 to 19 minutes (for 2½-inch cups) or until cupcakes spring back when lightly touched. Cool completely in pans on wire rack. Frost, if desired.

Makes 14 (2¾-inch) cupcakes

Chocolate-Cherry Cupcakes

2 eggs
⅔ cup buttermilk
¼ cup vegetable oil
1 teaspoon vanilla
1 jar Chocolate-Cherry Cupcake Mix
Frosting (optional)

1. Preheat oven to 350°F. Line 14 (2¾-inch) or 18 (2½-inch) muffin cups with paper or foil liners.
2. Beat eggs in small bowl; stir in buttermilk, oil and vanilla.
3. Place contents of jar in large bowl. Add egg mixture; beat on medium speed of electric mixer 1½ to 2 minutes or until blended. Spoon batter into muffin cups, filling ¾ full. Bake 20 to 21 minutes (for 2¾-inch cups) or 17 to 19 minutes (for 2½-inch cups) or until cupcakes spring back when lightly touched. Cool completely in pans on wire rack. Frost, if desired.

Makes 14 (2¾-inch) cupcakes

Chocolate-Cherry Cupcakes

2 eggs
⅔ cup buttermilk
¼ cup vegetable oil
1 teaspoon vanilla
1 jar Chocolate-Cherry Cupcake Mix
Frosting (optional)

1. Preheat oven to 350°F. Line 14 (2¾-inch) or 18 (2½-inch) muffin cups with paper or foil liners.
2. Beat eggs in small bowl; stir in buttermilk, oil and vanilla.
3. Place contents of jar in large bowl. Add egg mixture; beat on medium speed of electric mixer 1½ to 2 minutes or until blended. Spoon batter into muffin cups, filling ¾ full. Bake 20 to 21 minutes (for 2¾-inch cups) or 17 to 19 minutes (for 2½-inch cups) or until cupcakes spring back when lightly touched. Cool completely in pans on wire rack. Frost, if desired.

Makes 14 (2¾-inch) cupcakes

Chocolate-Cherry Cupcakes

2 eggs
⅔ cup buttermilk
¼ cup vegetable oil
1 teaspoon vanilla
1 jar Chocolate-Cherry Cupcake Mix
Frosting (optional)

1. Preheat oven to 350°F. Line 14 (2¾-inch) or 18 (2½-inch) muffin cups with paper or foil liners.
2. Beat eggs in small bowl; stir in buttermilk, oil and vanilla.
3. Place contents of jar in large bowl. Add egg mixture; beat on medium speed of electric mixer 1½ to 2 minutes or until blended. Spoon batter into muffin cups, filling ¾ full. Bake 20 to 21 minutes (for 2¾-inch cups) or 17 to 19 minutes (for 2½-inch cups) or until cupcakes spring back when lightly touched. Cool completely in pans on wire rack. Frost, if desired.

Makes 14 (2¾-inch) cupcakes

Chocolate-Cherry Cupcakes

2 eggs
⅔ cup buttermilk
¼ cup vegetable oil
1 teaspoon vanilla
1 jar Chocolate-Cherry Cupcake Mix
Frosting (optional)

1. Preheat oven to 350°F. Line 14 (2¾-inch) or 18 (2½-inch) muffin cups with paper or foil liners.
2. Beat eggs in small bowl; stir in buttermilk, oil and vanilla.
3. Place contents of jar in large bowl. Add egg mixture; beat on medium speed of electric mixer 1½ to 2 minutes or until blended. Spoon batter into muffin cups, filling ¾ full. Bake 20 to 21 minutes (for 2¾-inch cups) or 17 to 19 minutes (for 2½-inch cups) or until cupcakes spring back when lightly touched. Cool completely in pans on wire rack. Frost, if desired.

Makes 14 (2¾-inch) cupcakes

Cinnamon-Raisin Muffin Mix

- 1/3 cup granulated sugar
- 1/3 cup packed brown sugar
- 1 1/4 cups all-purpose flour
- 1 1/2 teaspoon baking powder
- 1 teaspoon ground cinnamon
- 1/2 teaspoon ground allspice
- 1/2 teaspoon ground nutmeg
- 1/4 teaspoon salt
- 1 cup uncooked quick oats
- 1 cup raisins

Layer ingredients in 1-quart food storage jar with tight-fitting lid in following order: granulated sugar; brown sugar, lightly packed; combined flour, baking powder, cinnamon, allspice, nutmeg and salt; oats; and raisins. Seal jar; cover lid with fabric. Attach gift tag and fabric to jar with raffia. *Makes one 1-quart jar*

Cinnamon-Raisin Muffins

⅓ cup butter
⅔ cup milk
1 egg
1 jar Cinnamon-Raisin Muffin Mix

1. Preheat oven to 400°F. Grease twelve 2½-inch muffin cups or line with paper or foil bake cups; set aside.

2. Place butter in medium microwavable bowl. Microwave about 45 seconds or until butter is melted; cool slightly. Add milk and egg; whisk until well blended.

3. Place contents of jar in separate medium bowl; stir until combined. Add butter mixture; stir until just blended. Fill prepared muffin cups ⅔ full with batter. Bake 14 to 15 minutes or until toothpick inserted in centers comes out clean. Cool 15 minutes in pan on wire rack; remove muffins from pan. Serve warm or at room temperature.

Makes 12 muffins

Cinnamon-Raisin Muffins

⅓ cup butter
⅔ cup milk
1 egg
1 jar Cinnamon-Raisin Muffin Mix

1. Preheat oven to 400°F. Grease twelve 2½-inch muffin cups or line with paper or foil bake cups; set aside.

2. Place butter in medium microwavable bowl. Microwave about 45 seconds or until butter is melted; cool slightly. Add milk and egg; whisk until well blended.

3. Place contents of jar in separate medium bowl; stir until combined. Add butter mixture; stir until just blended. Fill prepared muffin cups ⅔ full with batter. Bake 14 to 15 minutes or until toothpick inserted in centers comes out clean. Cool 15 minutes in pan on wire rack; remove muffins from pan. Serve warm or at room temperature. *Makes 12 muffins*

Cinnamon-Raisin Muffins

⅓ cup butter
⅔ cup milk
1 egg
1 jar Cinnamon-Raisin Muffin Mix

1. Preheat oven to 400°F. Grease twelve 2½-inch muffin cups or line with paper or foil bake cups; set aside.

2. Place butter in medium microwavable bowl. Microwave about 45 seconds or until butter is melted; cool slightly. Add milk and egg; whisk until well blended.

3. Place contents of jar in separate medium bowl; stir until combined. Add butter mixture; stir until just blended. Fill prepared muffin cups ⅔ full with batter. Bake 14 to 15 minutes or until toothpick inserted in centers comes out clean. Cool 15 minutes in pan on wire rack; remove muffins from pan. Serve warm or at room temperature. *Makes 12 muffins*

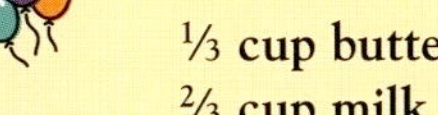

Cinnamon-Raisin Muffins

⅓ cup butter
⅔ cup milk
1 egg
1 jar Cinnamon-Raisin Muffin Mix

1. Preheat oven to 400°F. Grease twelve 2½-inch muffin cups or line with paper or foil bake cups; set aside.

2. Place butter in medium microwavable bowl. Microwave about 45 seconds or until butter is melted; cool slightly. Add milk and egg; whisk until well blended.

3. Place contents of jar in separate medium bowl; stir until combined. Add butter mixture; stir until just blended. Fill prepared muffin cups ⅔ full with batter. Bake 14 to 15 minutes or until toothpick inserted in centers comes out clean. Cool 15 minutes in pan on wire rack; remove muffins from pan. Serve warm or at room temperature. *Makes 12 muffins*

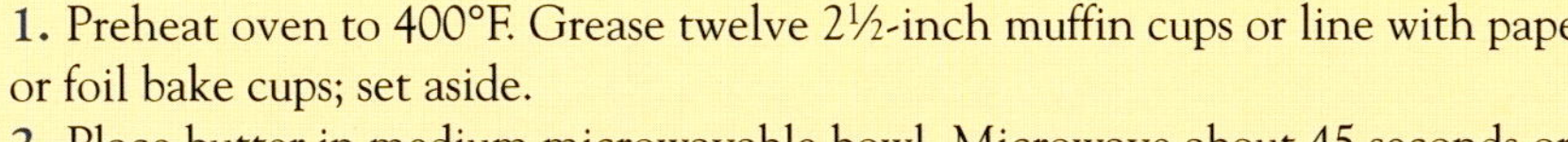

Cinnamon-Raisin Muffins

⅓ cup butter
⅔ cup milk
1 egg
1 jar Cinnamon-Raisin Muffin Mix

1. Preheat oven to 400°F. Grease twelve 2½-inch muffin cups or line with paper or foil bake cups; set aside.

2. Place butter in medium microwavable bowl. Microwave about 45 seconds or until butter is melted; cool slightly. Add milk and egg; whisk until well blended.

3. Place contents of jar in separate medium bowl; stir until combined. Add butter mixture; stir until just blended. Fill prepared muffin cups ⅔ full with batter. Bake 14 to 15 minutes or until toothpick inserted in centers comes out clean. Cool 15 minutes in pan on wire rack; remove muffins from pan. Serve warm or at room temperature.

Makes 12 muffins

Cinnamon-Raisin Muffins

⅓ cup butter
⅔ cup milk
1 egg
1 jar Cinnamon-Raisin Muffin Mix

1. Preheat oven to 400°F. Grease twelve 2½-inch muffin cups or line with paper or foil bake cups; set aside.

2. Place butter in medium microwavable bowl. Microwave about 45 seconds or until butter is melted; cool slightly. Add milk and egg; whisk until well blended.

3. Place contents of jar in separate medium bowl; stir until combined. Add butter mixture; stir until just blended. Fill prepared muffin cups ⅔ full with batter. Bake 14 to 15 minutes or until toothpick inserted in centers comes out clean. Cool 15 minutes in pan on wire rack; remove muffins from pan. Serve warm or at room temperature.

Makes 12 muffins

Cinnamon-Raisin Muffins

⅓ cup butter
⅔ cup milk
1 egg
1 jar Cinnamon-Raisin Muffin Mix

1. Preheat oven to 400°F. Grease twelve 2½-inch muffin cups or line with paper or foil bake cups; set aside.

2. Place butter in medium microwavable bowl. Microwave about 45 seconds or until butter is melted; cool slightly. Add milk and egg; whisk until well blended.

3. Place contents of jar in separate medium bowl; stir until combined. Add butter mixture; stir until just blended. Fill prepared muffin cups ⅔ full with batter. Bake 14 to 15 minutes or until toothpick inserted in centers comes out clean. Cool 15 minutes in pan on wire rack; remove muffins from pan. Serve warm or at room temperature.

Makes 12 muffins

Peanut Butter Chocolate Thumbprint Cookie Mix

- ⅔ cup granulated sugar
- ⅔ cup packed brown sugar
- 2 cups all-purpose flour
- ½ teaspoon salt
- ⅔ cup unsweetened cocoa powder

Layer ingredients in 1-quart food storage jar with tight-fitting lid in following order: granulated sugar; brown sugar, lightly packed; combined flour and salt; and cocoa. Seal jar; cover lid with fabric. Attach gift tag and fabric to jar with raffia.

Makes one 1-quart jar

Gift Idea: Assemble a gift basket with a jar of Peanut Butter Chocolate Thumbprint Cookie Mix, a jar of creamy peanut butter and a bag of chocolate candy kisses.

Peanut Butter Chocolate Thumbprint Cookies

1 cup (2 sticks) butter, softened
1 jar Peanut Butter Chocolate Thumbprint Cookie Mix
2 eggs
⅔ cup creamy peanut butter
Chocolate candy kisses

1. Beat butter 1 minute in large bowl with electric mixer at medium speed. Add contents of jar and eggs. Beat at low speed 30 seconds. Beat 1½ to 2 minutes at medium speed or until well blended. Cover; refrigerate dough 1 hour.

2. Preheat oven to 350°F. Shape dough into 1-inch balls. Place balls 1½ inches apart on *ungreased* cookie sheets. Press thumb into center of balls. (Return remaining dough to refrigerator) Bake 10 to 11 minutes or until set. Repeat with remaining cookie dough.

3. Cool cookies 1 minute on cookie sheets; remove cookies to wire rack. Cool completely. Fill center of each cookie with about ½ teaspoon peanut butter. Top with candy.

Makes about 5 dozen cookies

Peanut Butter Chocolate Thumbprint Cookies

1 cup (2 sticks) butter, softened
1 jar Peanut Butter Chocolate Thumbprint Cookie Mix
2 eggs
⅔ cup creamy peanut butter
Chocolate candy kisses

1. Beat butter 1 minute in large bowl with electric mixer at medium speed. Add contents of jar and eggs. Beat at low speed 30 seconds. Beat 1½ to 2 minutes at medium speed or until well blended. Cover; refrigerate dough 1 hour.
2. Preheat oven to 350°F. Shape dough into 1-inch balls. Place balls 1½ inches apart on *ungreased* cookie sheets. Press thumb into center of balls. (Return remaining dough to refrigerator) Bake 10 to 11 minutes or until set. Repeat with remaining cookie dough.
3. Cool cookies 1 minute on cookie sheets; remove cookies to wire rack. Cool completely. Fill center of each cookie with about ½ teaspoon peanut butter. Top with candy.

Makes about 5 dozen cookies

Peanut Butter Chocolate Thumbprint Cookies

1 cup (2 sticks) butter, softened
1 jar Peanut Butter Chocolate Thumbprint Cookie Mix
2 eggs
⅔ cup creamy peanut butter
Chocolate candy kisses

1. Beat butter 1 minute in large bowl with electric mixer at medium speed. Add contents of jar and eggs. Beat at low speed 30 seconds. Beat 1½ to 2 minutes at medium speed or until well blended. Cover; refrigerate dough 1 hour.
2. Preheat oven to 350°F. Shape dough into 1-inch balls. Place balls 1½ inches apart on *ungreased* cookie sheets. Press thumb into center of balls. (Return remaining dough to refrigerator) Bake 10 to 11 minutes or until set. Repeat with remaining cookie dough.
3. Cool cookies 1 minute on cookie sheets; remove cookies to wire rack. Cool completely. Fill center of each cookie with about ½ teaspoon peanut butter. Top with candy.

Makes about 5 dozen cookies

Peanut Butter Chocolate Thumbprint Cookies

1 cup (2 sticks) butter, softened
1 jar Peanut Butter Chocolate Thumbprint Cookie Mix
2 eggs
⅔ cup creamy peanut butter
Chocolate candy kisses

1. Beat butter 1 minute in large bowl with electric mixer at medium speed. Add contents of jar and eggs. Beat at low speed 30 seconds. Beat 1½ to 2 minutes at medium speed or until well blended. Cover; refrigerate dough 1 hour.
2. Preheat oven to 350°F. Shape dough into 1-inch balls. Place balls 1½ inches apart on *ungreased* cookie sheets. Press thumb into center of balls. (Return remaining dough to refrigerator) Bake 10 to 11 minutes or until set. Repeat with remaining cookie dough.
3. Cool cookies 1 minute on cookie sheets; remove cookies to wire rack. Cool completely. Fill center of each cookie with about ½ teaspoon peanut butter. Top with candy.

Makes about 5 dozen cookies

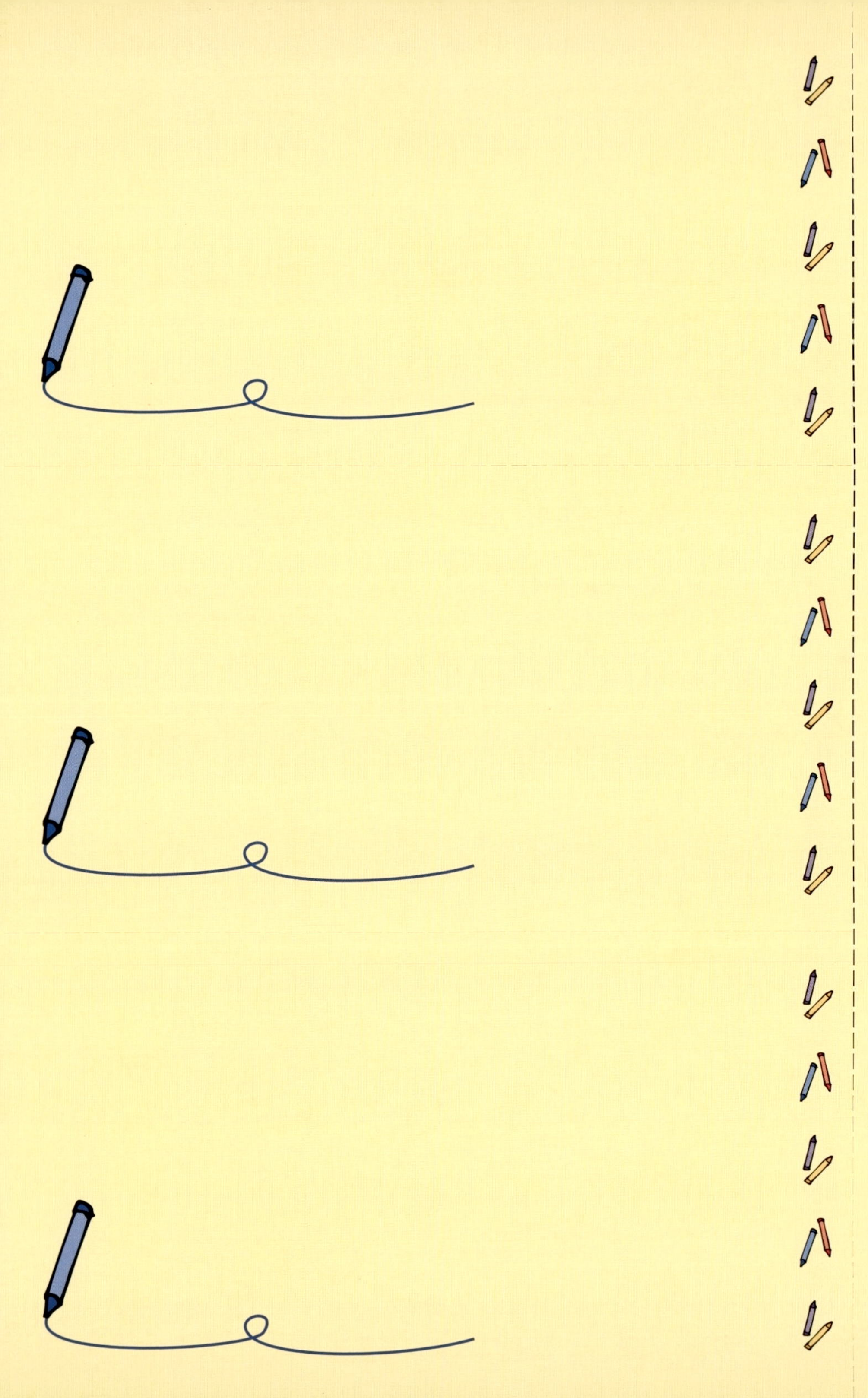

Peanut Butter Chocolate Thumbprint Cookies

1 cup (2 sticks) butter, softened
1 jar Peanut Butter Chocolate Thumbprint Cookie Mix
2 eggs
⅔ cup creamy peanut butter
Chocolate candy kisses

1. Beat butter 1 minute in large bowl with electric mixer at medium speed. Add contents of jar and eggs. Beat at low speed 30 seconds. Beat 1½ to 2 minutes at medium speed or until well blended. Cover; refrigerate dough 1 hour.
2. Preheat oven to 350°F. Shape dough into 1-inch balls. Place balls 1½ inches apart on *ungreased* cookie sheets. Press thumb into center of balls. (Return remaining dough to refrigerator) Bake 10 to 11 minutes or until set. Repeat with remaining cookie dough.
3. Cool cookies 1 minute on cookie sheets; remove cookies to wire rack. Cool completely. Fill center of each cookie with about ½ teaspoon peanut butter. Top with candy.

Makes about 5 dozen cookies

Peanut Butter Chocolate Thumbprint Cookies

1 cup (2 sticks) butter, softened
1 jar Peanut Butter Chocolate Thumbprint Cookie Mix
2 eggs
⅔ cup creamy peanut butter
Chocolate candy kisses

1. Beat butter 1 minute in large bowl with electric mixer at medium speed. Add contents of jar and eggs. Beat at low speed 30 seconds. Beat 1½ to 2 minutes at medium speed or until well blended. Cover; refrigerate dough 1 hour.
2. Preheat oven to 350°F. Shape dough into 1-inch balls. Place balls 1½ inches apart on *ungreased* cookie sheets. Press thumb into center of balls. (Return remaining dough to refrigerator) Bake 10 to 11 minutes or until set. Repeat with remaining cookie dough.
3. Cool cookies 1 minute on cookie sheets; remove cookies to wire rack. Cool completely. Fill center of each cookie with about ½ teaspoon peanut butter. Top with candy.

Makes about 5 dozen cookies

Peanut Butter Chocolate Thumbprint Cookies

1 cup (2 sticks) butter, softened
1 jar Peanut Butter Chocolate Thumbprint Cookie Mix
2 eggs
⅔ cup creamy peanut butter
Chocolate candy kisses

1. Beat butter 1 minute in large bowl with electric mixer at medium speed. Add contents of jar and eggs. Beat at low speed 30 seconds. Beat 1½ to 2 minutes at medium speed or until well blended. Cover; refrigerate dough 1 hour.
2. Preheat oven to 350°F. Shape dough into 1-inch balls. Place balls 1½ inches apart on *ungreased* cookie sheets. Press thumb into center of balls. (Return remaining dough to refrigerator) Bake 10 to 11 minutes or until set. Repeat with remaining cookie dough.
3. Cool cookies 1 minute on cookie sheets; remove cookies to wire rack. Cool completely. Fill center of each cookie with about ½ teaspoon peanut butter. Top with candy.

Makes about 5 dozen cookies

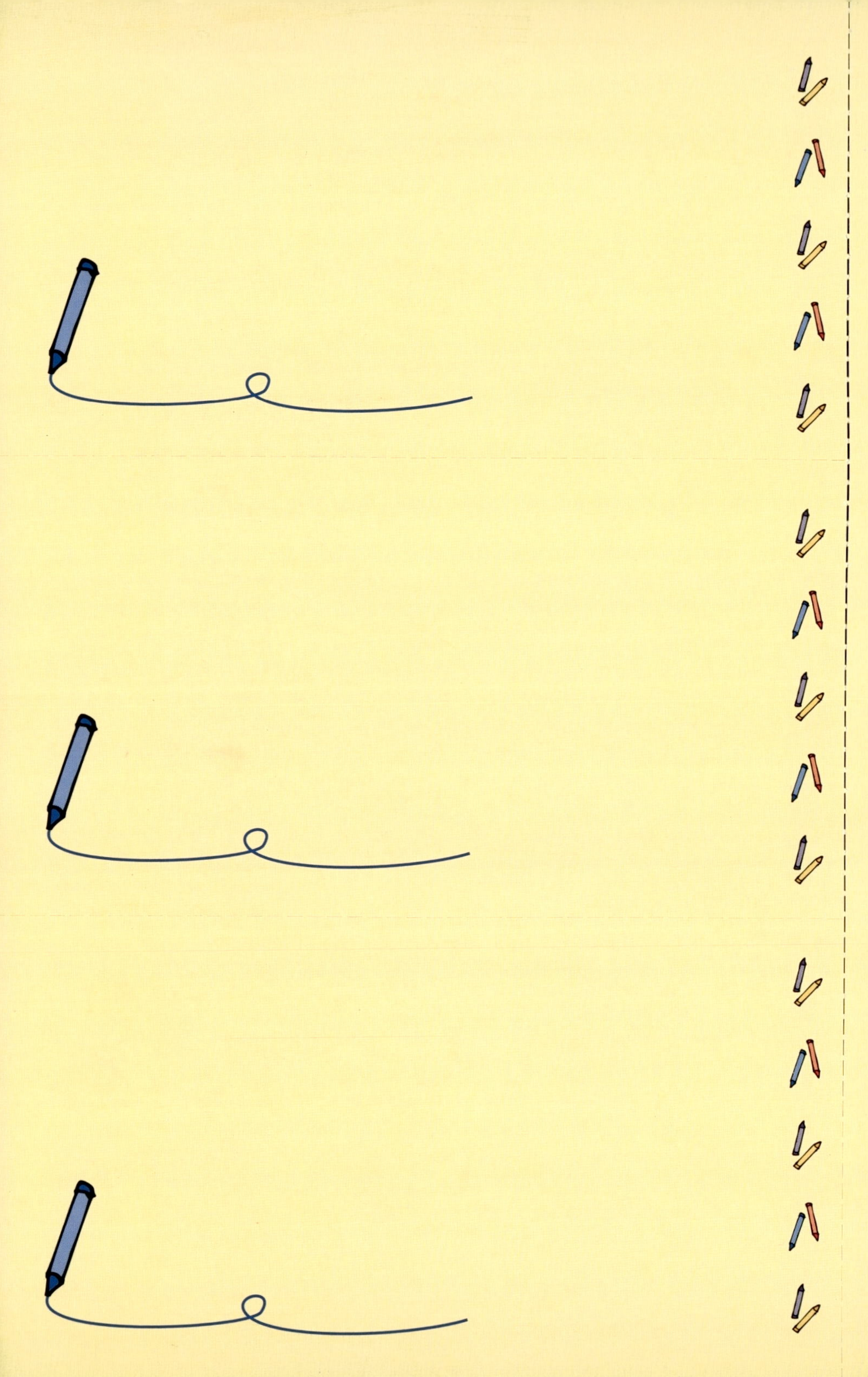